American

BURGER
REVIVAL

American
BURGER
REVIVAL

BRAZEN RECIPES TO ELECTRIFY
A TIMELESS CLASSIC

SAMUEL MONSOUR *and* **RICHARD CHUDY**

UNION PARK PRESS

BOSTON

Union Park Press
P.O. Box 81435
Wellesley, MA 02481
www.unionparkpress.com

Printed in China
First Edition

© 2015 Samuel Monsour and Richard Chudy

  Library of Congress Cataloging-in-Publication Data

Monsour Samuel.
  American burger revival : brazen recipes to electrify a timeless classic /Samuel Monsour
and Richard Chudy. -- First Edition.
       pages cm
  Includes bibliographical references and index.
  ISBN 978-1-934598-13-9 (alk. paper)
  1. Hamburgers. 2. Cooking, American. I. Chudy, Richard. II. Title.
  TX749.5.B43C49 2015
  641.3'62--dc23
                                   2014047157

ISBN: 978-1-934598-13-9

Book and cover design by Vale Hill Creative. **www.valehillcreative.com**

Photo credits: Unless noted otherwise, photography by Katie Chudy,
www.smallbostonkitchen.com

Photographs on pages *vi-vii, viii* (top), *ix, x, xviii,* 4-5, 6, 7, 8-9, 11, 12-13, 14, 18-19, 24-25, 34, 48
(top, middle), 72, 90, 95, 98-99, 103, 104-105, 108-109, 110, 111 (left), 123, 134, 136, 138, 160, 205,
206-207, 208, 214-215, 238-239 by Tara Morris, www.taramorrisimages.com

Photographs on pages *iv-v,* 38-39, 46 by Shelby Larsson

Photographs on page 169 © fragless/iStockPhoto.com

www.unionparkpress.com

  BOSTON

*To my wife Katie. For being there every step of the way, inspiring me,
believing in me, and kindly letting me know when I have cheese in my beard.*

– R.C.

*For Deborah, Astrid, Jenifer, Sammantha, Jo-Anna, Jessica, Lesley,
Rose, and especially Jeanne. If it weren't for the unconditional love and support
that all of you very special ladies have constantly sprinkled into my life,
my food would most certainly lack flavor and soul.*

– S.M.

TABLE OF CONTENTS

INTRODUCTION

I was always that dumb kid ordering a burger at restaurants when it didn't make sense. While it turns out that Papa Gino's, with its famed Papa Burger (complete with a tabletop Pac-Man game), may not be the ideal spot for a burger fix, I knew at a young age that the burger was the perfect food. Burgers growing up were solid; my mom will tell you I always preferred the pre-formed hockey puck burgers found at every supermarket in the country over the homemade ones she lovingly crafted for us. To my untrained palate, fast food burgers were just fine; my first In-n-Out was a revelation, and the first time I sat down with my future wife over a juicy burger is a moment I will never forget.

During my senior year of college, after a long and painful period living off ten-cent ramen noodles and cafeteria food, I had finally had enough and decided to take matters into my own hands. Armed with a handful of new cookbooks (that I'd probably be ashamed to claim as my own now) and a VHS cassette of Food Network and PBS cooking shows, I tried my hand at cooking. After a series of late-night, après-bar shame meals, I began experimenting, cooking meals for my roommates, JP, Jon, and James. For our last college party I manned the kitchen with James, mixing up burgers that somehow developed a legendary status. The satisfaction we felt after serving what I still consider to be some of my finest burger creations will never leave me. I will always remember that moment when the smell of grease, cheap beer, and good

company seemed to encapsulate all that was right with the world. My love for the burger has only grown, and my one hope is that everyone can experience burger nirvana like I did on that fateful day in the middle of nowhere, New Hampshire.

-RICHARD

. . . .

When I was in my early twenties, I lived in the Hudson Valley and frequently made brief treks to Manhattan with hopes of satiating my appetite for food and dining. I was lucky enough to have a close friend that lived in Chelsea who cooked for Jean-Georges Vongerichten. She knew the scene well, and with her as my guide, I had some great eats. We devoured a vast range of food in a variety of atmospheres, from ketchup and caviar to dim sum and tapas, in dive bars and joints boasting Michelin stars. I had an incredible amount of thought-provoking experiences, but to this day, the most unexpected and momentous bite I've taken was at the Corner Bistro in the West Village.

I vividly remember the details. The exterior was dingy, with a generic neon sign hanging outside. Everything was worn, black, and tatted up with graffiti. The service staff was either young and hip or old as dirt. The burgers were five bucks and the beers were three. This place was authentic as shit, and as a dive bar enthusiast, I knew I was in for a treat.

We ordered our burgers medium rare, and they arrived eight minutes later, blasting hot with a rich Maillard crust. The burgers were thick and juicy, served on a sesame seed bun with yellow American cheese, crispy bacon, and salad bar fixin's. The first bite was so damn good that I was instantly brought back to my roots.

Now, as I look back, I see that these types of food memories are what inspire my cuisine. More often than not, it's the dishes I grew up learning to cook alongside my father at our family's neighborhood bar and grill in Chapel Hill, North Carolina that I'm most proud of. The burger is my safe place, where I feel most comfortable—the dish I find endlessly inspiring. It's the canvas I want to paint.

The burger was always a staple in our restaurant and something that Pops took great pride in. My father and I can talk about burgers for hours. It's what we plan vacation itineraries around and what satisfies our souls more than anything else. The burger: a global icon of American cuisine. I promise to cook, eat, honor, and celebrate you with great pride and joy for the rest of my life.

-SAMMY

HOW TO USE THIS COOKBOOK

We get it, you loathe mustard (weirdo) or maybe pork belly isn't your thing (we'll look the other way). But one thing we can all agree on is the power of the burger, and we've outlined a myriad of recipes and techniques—some of them outrageous, a few expected—that will make you glad you're here. We wholeheartedly encourage you to build your own flavor profiles, dazzle your guests with your own interpretations, and eat that filthy burger at ungodly hours if you so desire. We won't judge you for gorging on Peameal Bacon for breakfast or drinking Umami Ketchup from your hipster mason jar. In fact, we love it, we do it too, and hopefully we will inspire you to take your next burger to whatever level you please.

But we can't just leave you out in the cold either, can we? With a few calculated exceptions we provide pairings for interesting creations for every recipe in this book. Additionally, we have included a baker's dozen of composed sandwiches (we call them Centerfolds, but don't tell our wives) that hopefully whet your appetite to create the most extreme burger possible. Use them for inspiration. It should also be said that we don't expect you to use this (ahem, mind-blowing) cookbook only for crafting burgers—these recipes are versatile and delicious, and we know you'll find *plenty* of ways to use them. Be bold. Be playful. Choose your own adventure. And delight in it.

IT'S FUNNY TO THINK there can be so much to say about something as seemingly straightforward as the humble burger, but when it comes to Americans and their national dish, entire bookshelves could be filled with discussions on the matter. In fact, the burger is such a seminal element of American cookery it deserves a meaty manifesto. So here is ours.

Consider the following evidence:

HISTORY: Burgers have been around since the beginning of time (or close to it) and pretty much everybody loves to eat them.

ECONOMICS: Burgers have long been an affordable option at lunch counters, fast food joints, and backyard cookouts around the country.

ART: Burgers are an excellent vehicle for creativity and experimentation.

MATH: While other food fads have come and gone, burgers have withstood the test of time and even continue to gain popularity; Americans consume 135 million burgers every single day.

AND PERHAPS MOST IMPORTANTLY: Burgers are extremely tasty.

It's for all those reasons that we're in the midst of a burger renaissance, a *revival* if you will. Chefs and home cooks alike are thinking about their burgers in a new way. Sure, two all-beef patties, special sauce, lettuce, cheese, pickles, onions, and a sesame seed bun may have done the trick in the past—but why not try something a little more adventurous? That's exactly what has happened in recent years as well-regarded chefs from coast to coast offer gourmet burgers on their menus, providing inventive takes on the beloved classic.

Want to know why? Because you have to give the people what they want. And the people want burgers, dammit! Chefs are combining their creativity with well-honed skills and carefully sourced ingredients to elevate this sandwich with tremendous results. The burger is as comfortable in a fine dining restaurant as it is in your neighborhood pub, and professional kitchens are creating unforgettable meals for carnivores everywhere.

These perfectly juicy burgers with well-seasoned crusts and outrageous toppings have upped the game. Why not put a brisket-short rib blend on a handcrafted bun? Would you like to add a fried egg? How about pork belly and the house-fermented pickles? Nothing is off limits. Everything is possible. And that's what this revival (and book) is all about.

American Burger Revival is not for lazy motherfuckers. This cookbook is for those who are dedicated and devoted to their burgers. This book is for the highly motivated, flavor-obsessed, red-blooded, red-meat-loving home cooks across this great land. It's for those who enjoy the time they spend preparing a fine sandwich. The folks who take pride in knowing they can make anything and everything from scratch—from grinding their own perfectly balanced blend of meat to waiting twenty-eight days for the best damn pickle they've ever tasted. Keep in mind that it's not enough to just *make* everything—it actually has to taste great, too. Cooking tasty food requires a lot of love, care, attention, experience, and more often than not, knowledge.

As professional chefs, we prepare everything from scratch using whole ingredients and a whole lot of tenderness. Except when we don't, and then we go full force in the other direction and play around with things like instant gravy packets, mac and cheese powder, and crushed corn chips. You know, for balance. Some people might say we take a high-low approach. We like to think we just make delicious food.

We've spent the better portion of our careers thinking about, eating, and preparing innovative burgers that push the limits of expectations. We have discovered tried and true techniques that work and have spent years experimenting with flavor profiles and textures that complement the rich quality of a well-made patty. Our goal is to show you that you're just as badass as the next guy or gal so that you can bring the sophisticated flavors and skills of your favorite eatery to your own kitchen or backyard.

So a few things to think about as we start this journey together: When it comes to creating the perfect patty there is no excuse not to source the best meat possible. If you're up for grinding your own beef, then do so thoughtfully. Think about the blend. Are you going for straight up chuck? Or do you want to experiment with a different mix? How about texture? Do you like a finely ground melt-in-your-mouth feel? Or do you want something steaky, with more heft and chew to it? We're going to walk you through the secret tradecraft of hamburgery. When to flip and how. Whether to grill or griddle. The ins and outs of righteous meat-to-bun ratios. And how to season your meat like it's got something to say.

After the patty, the game is on and the world is your oyster (a Johnnycake Fried Oyster to be exact, see page 211.) Instead of giving you a series of top-down sandwiches, we're providing you with an arsenal of recipes to develop and create your own dream burger. The bulk of this cookbook focuses on the components you'll want to add to your burger and for good reason. Your brilliant patty deserves some personality. Some flavor. Some culture.

We dedicate a serious amount of ink to making homemade buns, decadent cheese creations, and craft condiments that have their own stories to tell. We present to you pages and pages of pickles and a whole slew of edible delights that defy categorization, so we begged our publishers to add them to a chapter named for our favorite part of the kitchen: the junk drawer. Many of the recipes in this book are so damn good they could (and should) stand alone as dishes in their own right. Lowcountry Cornbread. Vermont "Velveeta." Fried Ketchup. Hushpuppy Battered Rellenos. Smoked Tasso Ham. These are the reasons life is worth living. Stack them high on your next burger, however, and you might just find some religion.

Stoke the coals, fire up your imagination, and prepare to see the light.

CHEFS' NOTES

FRYING GUIDE

More than a few of our recipes require a skinny dip in a vat of oil. Below we've outlined the steps for frying success.

When choosing frying oil, opt for a fat with a high smoke point. Our three favorites are:

Extra light olive oil (465°F smoke point)

Peanut oil (450°F smoke point)

Canola oil (400°F smoke point)

Their high smoke points make them ideal for frying and other high-heat cooking methods, such as sautéing, roasting, and grilling. We highly recommend that you pick quality oils from reputable sources to ensure consistent results.

EQUIPMENT

If using a deep fryer:

We recommend using an 8- or 12-cup tabletop electric deep fryer. (They're usually priced at $30 and up.)

Fill your deep fryer with the recommended amount of frying oil and set it to the desired temperature. Hold off on frying until the oil is the correct temperature and follow recipe instructions.

Carefully place whatever you are frying into the hot oil. Allow for plenty of personal space between items; don't let anything touch.

If you're frying in multiple batches, bring the oil back up to the original temperature (it will cool down in between batches) before placing the next batch in the oil.

If frying in a pot:

Use the largest heavy-bottomed pot you have and keep a candy thermometer at the ready.

Follow the same steps as you would when frying in a tabletop deep fryer. You need to be extra careful and make sure you don't add so much oil to the pot that it overflows. (This will create a mess and burn your skin off.) Our recipes suggest using 4 cups of oil, but be smart about this! Because pot sizes vary, here is a good rule of thumb: only fill your pot halfway with oil.

TEMPERATURE CONTROL AND CONSISTENCY

Whether you're frying in a tabletop contraption or a pot, always fry with a thermometer. This will allow you to accurately and safely keep an eye on your oil temperature. If your oil is too hot, your food will burn and most likely explode (see above about the mess/burn warnings). If you're using a pot, the best way to avoid overheating your oil is to use a candy thermometer. They're equipped to latch onto the side of a pot and will typically read temperatures up to 400°F. A good one will cost you $10.

VACUUM SEALING

Relax; you don't need NASA training to use a vacuum sealer. You're probably familiar with its more commonly known household name, a food saver. This handy little device uses a vacuum to create a zero-air atmosphere for your food, and then it creates an airtight seal. Simple as that.

Your next question is probably: why should I bother? Well, air causes all sorts of foul stuff to go down, like spoilage, loss of flavor, and freezer burn. Vacuum sealing will save your food from these atrocities, increase the shelf life of the product while in the refrigerator or freezer, eliminate the chance of funky fridge odor absorption, and make deep-freezer dehydration via oxidation impossible.

In this book, we mainly use the vacuum sealer when preparing sous vide items. Vacuum sealing in commercial-grade vacuum sealer bags is the industry standard for this particular method of cookery, and we prefer to stick to the script. If you don't have a vacuum sealer but you'd still like to sous vide, don't sweat it. Simply use a 1-gallon freezer-strength resealable bag. Make sure to squeeze out as much air as possible and double check that there are no small openings in the seal before submerging your package into a water bath.

SOUS VIDE COOKING

Sous vide cooking is just pompous French talk for "cooking under vacuum." It's really just a more precise crockpot. But with precision comes accuracy, and with accuracy comes difficulty. Like many techniques, sous vide cooking requires a skill set.

However, there are tons of resources available to help you get there. And if you love nerding out like we do, it will prove to be a truly rewarding party trick.

Sous vide cooking entails vacuum sealing your food, submerging the food into a circulating water bath, and then precisely maintaining the temperature of the water. This method heats the food evenly while allowing it to retain its moisture. Sous vide cooking usually takes much longer than traditional cooking methods, but the results are nearly always worth the wait.

In order to effectively sous vide, follow these general steps:

❶ Determine the temperature and time of your cooking process.

❷ Chances are you'll be using a machine that you submerge into a water bath. Choose a bath large enough to accommodate the food you'll be cooking (a large stock pot, 5-gallon bucket, etc.). Once submerged, set your machine to the desired temperature.

❸ Vacuum seal the food to be cooked.

❹ Once the water bath has reached the desired temperature, gently submerge your vacuum-sealed food.

❺ Allow the water to circulate for the determined time.

There are manufacturers offering sous vide machines for the household cook for about $100, but we highly recommend spending a few more bucks and getting a sous vide machine from Polyscience—a

Ragin' Cajun

The Nacho libre

The Mac Mayor

leader in this technology. They offer reliable sous vide machines and vacuum sealers for every budget and purpose.

SMOKERS

The world of smoking and smoking tools is big enough to fill an entire book, so we'll keep it short.

We love smoking foods. The act. The aroma. The flavor. To us, there is nothing better than a perfectly smoked... anything. There is also nothing worse or more disappointing than foods that are improperly smoked, whether they barely taste of smoke or they're dried out and bitter. You can obtain perfection by choosing the right tools. We have tested a few well-regarded smokers and here are our favorites. The main difference is price and ambition.

THE CAMERON SMOKER

This stovetop option makes for a great introductory smoker and is easy to keep around the house. It retails for about $50 and can serve as your gateway drug. It might fill your home with black smoke from time to time, but we're sure your neighbors won't mind. (Just give them some of that Smoked Tasso Ham on page 214 and they'll understand).

THE POLYSCIENCE SMOKING GUN

This is a very fun tool to have in your kitchen. This battery-powered gun allows for the application of cool smoke, which translates into big flavor. For around $100, you'll be experimenting with smoke not only in your burgers, but also with your vegetables, chocolate, and cocktails.

THE BRADLEY ORIGINAL SMOKER

For the more serious home-smoking aficionado, we highly recommend the Bradley Original Smoker. Its electronically controlled temperature range can be set from low to high, which represents ambient to 250°F. For fuel, this smoker uses Bradley's signature hardwood bisquettes. They're available in twelve varieties, including Hickory, Alder, and Pecan, and each bisquette burns for thirty minutes. For just under $300, you can get a smoker that gets going quickly and works on an automatic feed, so all you've got to do is keep your eye on the clock and guzzle cold beer.

TSM 20 POUND DIGITAL SMOKER

Jumping up in capability, output, sturdiness, and price, we also got our hands on a four rack, 20-pound digital smoker designed and manufactured by The Sausage Maker, based out of Buffalo, New York. (The "20-pound" refers to how much meat you can smoke per batch.)

Its heating cabinet is set by a digital temperature control, allowing complete accuracy for setting a temperature range between 50°F and 200°F. It uses saw dust for smoking, which is inexpensive and easy to find (in hardware stores and on the internet). For $800, you're not just buying a backyard smoker. This precise, all stainless steel smoker is NSF approved, making it legal for commercial usage. If smoking is just a hobby, this smoker is not for you. But if you've ever dreamed of entering into barbecue contests or selling some pulled pork sandwiches at a farmers market for a little extra weekend scratch, this piece of equipment will help you get there.

1.
THE MEAT OF THE MATTER

THE AMERICAN BURGER REVIVAL begins with the perfect patty. Last time we checked, hamburgers were made out of beef, so that's the script we're sticking to. Not that turkey-burger-seared-salmon-roasted-mushroom-cap poser bullshit. Nope. When it comes down to it, beef is the meat of the matter.

To us, the perfect burger is loaded with toppings, sauces, and cheese, but if the patty isn't impeccable, your burger will never live up to its juicy, beefy, satisfying potential. But just like the endless array of toppings available to you, there are wonderful variations worth exploring when it comes to selecting which cuts of beef to use when forming your patties. There's nothing wrong with chuck, but adding other cuts can change the flavor profile of your burger in ways you never imagined.

If you only pay attention to one chapter in this cookbook, it should be this one. In the pages that follow, we outline the right beef to buy and list the proper cuts to use when grinding your own meat. We'll tackle the hot-button issues head on: the perfect patty size, grill versus griddle, when to flip and how, when to season, and why to rest. This is where it all starts. Welcome to burgernomics.

STORE-GROUND BEEF

There's nothing wrong with buying store-ground beef, but you should know what you're looking for. After many years of sourcing quality products, deliberation, and debate, here are the guidelines we follow:

Only buy beef that clearly states the breed of cattle (Black Angus, Hereford, Piedmontese, Wagyu, etc.).

Only buy beef that was ground within the past twenty-four hours.

For optimal flavor and juiciness, make sure you have a protein-to-fat ratio of 80/20, respectively.

Seek out beef that has been raised naturally and, preferably, local to you.

Never use beef that was frozen after grinding.

Never use pre-made patties.

If it meets all these requirements, we absolutely love 100 percent ground chuck.

HOME-GROUND BEEF

If you've got the burger basics down and are looking to step up your game, home-ground beef is the way to go. Grinding your own beef has many merits. Besides giving you bragging rights, home-ground beef has an indescribable freshness that will enhance your burger's succulence. The flavor profiles of beef vary greatly from cut to cut; once you get into the world of grinding and mixing different cuts, you'll experience a new level of burger making that will blow you and your friends away.

CREATING YOUR OWN BLEND

No matter what cuts you mix and match, the key to successful beef-grinding alchemy is to concoct a grind with an overall protein-to-fat ratio of 80/20. As long as you maintain this ratio, you can stick with a simple one-cut grind or get real complicated and craft a grind of two, three, four, or even five cuts—it's totally your call.

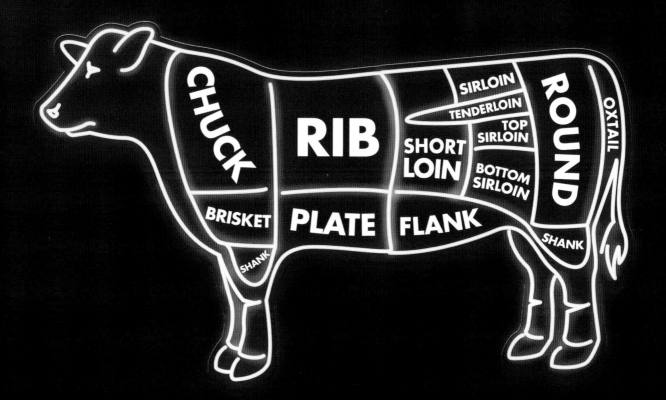

CHUCK (80/20): When old-school butchers refer to "hamburg," they're speaking of chuck, and even more specifically, chuck roll. It's as classic as you can get, yielding a high-fat burger that comes across as juicy rather than greasy. Most ground beef—and burgers—come from the chuck, so this cut is an obvious choice. Hands down, it's our favorite cut to grind. At the grocery store, look for the slab labeled "chuck pot roast." Grind it up and you'll instantly think *burger*.

BRISKET (70/30): This blue-collar cut is popular for boiled dinners, delicatessens, and barbecue joints. Its distinct flavor profile and high-fat content will yield a rich burger with a humble meat-and-potatoes attitude.

RIB (70/30): Another high-fat cut, this primal slab produces some real burger beauties. Our favorite rib cuts for grinding are short rib, flanken, and ribeye cap.

PLATE (90/10): The plate is just below the ribs. This cut yields both skirt and hanger steaks. These are slightly tougher cuts with buttery yet tangy flavor profiles, similar to the strong malolactic notes of a tart, velvety red wine. The sophisticated flavors of the plate lend themselves nicely to a fancier burger night.

SHORT LOIN (85/15): If you win the lottery (and suddenly feel like a ridiculous asshole), we recommend sourcing our favorite cut from the short loin: a dry-aged New York strip steak. Dry aging produces an umami-packed profile that comes from an enzymatic breakdown of muscle. You just can't find that flavor anywhere else. Most importantly, dry aging yields the amino acid glutamate. (It's the same glutamate found in monosodium glutamate— *the dreaded MSG!*—that buzz that Chinese take-out provides without the cancer scare.) So if you've got money to burn and you're looking for a burger to give you some zip, this cut is for you.

FLANK (93/7): Remember when London broil was cheap? We do. Back then, chefs were doing tasty things with flank, like marinating, charring, and shaving it so thin the meat just melted in your mouth. Even though the price of this cut has skyrocketed in the last ten years, it's still a worthwhile component in your burger blend. That's right, bring back the London broil, baby!

SIRLOIN (85/15): The sirloin can be complicated. There's sirloin, tenderloin, top sirloin, and bottom sirloin. Flavors and marbling vary greatly throughout the sirloin region, so for burger-grinding purposes, we suggest sticking to the bottom. Bottom sirloin is well marbled and packed with two of our favorite cuts, both for grilling and grinding: flap meat, also known as steak tips (and typically only available on the East Coast) and tri-tip (usually only available on the West Coast).

ROUND (96/7): Cuts from the round are lean and cheap. They're a great go-to when you need to adjust your protein-to-fat ratio. Typical cuts include top round, bottom round, and eye round.

SHANK (96/4): The shank is cut from either the hind shank or fore shank (or the calves and forearms). These muscles are constantly used, which gives them a beefy flavor but a tough consistency. Such tough cuts tend to be best for braising, but remember, a few grinds of even the toughest meats will yield a tender, melt-in-your-mouth texture. We love the shank because it adds a rich and gelatinous beefiness to our burgers. Be sure to pair this lean cut with fattier cuts.

OXTAIL (85/15): Sometimes we just love getting funky with our burger grinds. That's where oxtail comes in. Similar to the shank, this cut is very tough and gelatinous. It's also high in fat and low in cost. Pick up some tail next time you want to try something a little different.

HEAD: Leave it for braising or barbacoa.

YOU'VE JUST TAKEN a crash course on almost everything there is to know about cuts of beef. The important thing is to use this information as a guideline and have some fun. Here are a few examples of some of our all-star burger blends.

CHARLES BARKLEY A.K.A SIR CHARLES (50% Sirloin and 50% Chuck)

If you aren't going with just sirloin or just chuck, combining the two is the next logical step. Flap meat (from the bottom sirloin) is well marbled and breaks down nicely in a grinder, while chuck will give you that classic burger flavor profile that's hard to beat.

MUGGSY BOGUES (70% Short Rib and 30% Shank)

Don't let the little guy fool you. Much like the shortest man to ever play in the NBA, this combo is a force to be reckoned with. Short rib might be short, but it's about as marbled a cut as you can get. The muscle's constant action makes this cut packed with flavor. This robust blend has a ton of personality with grassy, sweet undertones.

DENNIS RODMAN (33% Oxtail, 33% Skirt Steak and 33% Brisket)

An odd combo, maybe, but the zany, skirt-wearing legend inspired this trio, and we think you'll dig it. It's got depth, funk, and a unique beefiness that Rodman himself would endorse. Probably.

SCOTTIE PIPPEN (25% Hanger Steak, 25% Flank Steak and 50% Ribeye Cap)

The jack-of-all-trades burger, much like Pippen himself (born in *Hamburg*, AR by the way), does a little bit of everything and does it well. The fat from the ribeye cap is rounded out by the lean nature of the flank, and the hanger gives this blend a meaty depth.

GRIND TIME

Pull out your meat grinder and plug it in—it's time to grind!

STEP 1: *Freeze Your Equipment*

Everything in burgerland needs to be ice cold (beers included). This rule is particularly important when grinding your own meat. Be sure to throw all parts (except the electric base, professor) into your freezer for at least 30 minutes prior to grinding.

STEP 2: *Cube Beef*

While your equipment is chilling, take all the beautiful meat out of the fridge and begin cutting it into 1-inch cubes—they don't have to be perfect. Be sure to remove any sinew, silver skin, and tendon.

STEP 3: *Blast Chill Beef*

Once your meat is cubed, lay it evenly on a sheet tray and place it in the freezer until edges are firm to touch, about 20 to 30 minutes. Cold meat grinds smoothly while room-temperature meat gets pasty.

If you are using a wet seasoning, prepare the recipe and toss it with the cubed beef immediately before blast chilling.

STEP 4: *Choose Die Size*

Typically, there are 2 standard dies that come with a meat grinder. One is coarse, usually comprised of ⅜-inch sized holes, and one is fine, usually comprised of ⅛-inch sized holes. For a hearty,

almost steak-like burger, use the coarse die. For a traditional, more melt-in-your-mouth texture, the fine die will do the trick. Of course, there is room to play around here. You can mix half and half and find your own middle ground. (Pun intended.)

STEP 5: *Grind*

Set your grinder up with your die of choice, remove your meat from the freezer, and start stuffing your cubes through the grinder, catching all the beautifully ground beef in a bowl. Don't handle it too much once it's ground; let it gently fall into the bowl without using your hands if possible. Some people grind once, some grind twice, and old-school cats grind 3 times. For real. We're not sure that triple grinding is completely necessary, but we do recommend grinding your meat twice as it ensures tenderness and helps prevent crumbling.

ARE YOU IN the market for a grinder? We like the Mega-force from Mercantile Station 2 or the meat grinder attachment on a KitchenAid. Both are great options. If you already have a KitchenAid, the meat grinder attachment is a practical solution. If you want to take your grinding to the next level, spend a little more and go with a nice electronic grinder, like the Megaforce.

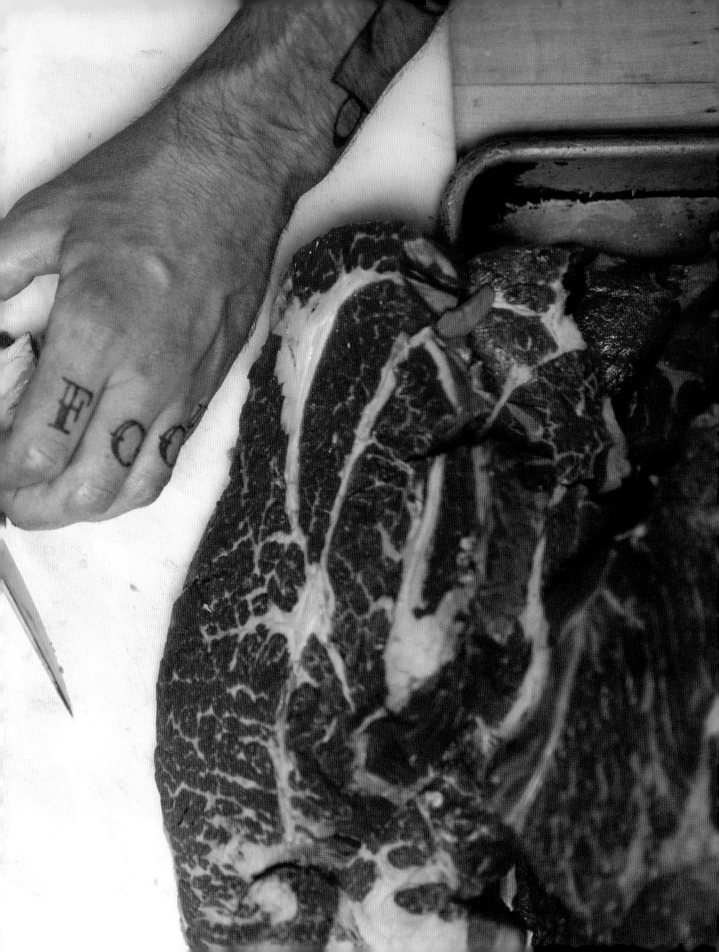

PATTY FORMATION

This is pretty simple—you know, as long as you follow our directions to the T.

If you are working with store-ground beef, now's the time to add a wet seasoning if you're so inclined. Simply mix in the wet seasoning before you begin to form your patties. You can even let the beef and seasoning hang out in the refrigerator for an hour so the flavors get to know each other. After that, proceed to form your patties.

Keep your meat as cold as ice before you start forming your patties, and don't over-manipulate the meat.

It is also important to keep a loose pack on the meat as this will result in a juicy, tender texture. Ever notice that pre-formed patties tend to be bouncy and dry? That texture occurs because the meat is overworked and packed too firmly, which basically creates an emulsion between the fat and meat similar to forcemeat.

NO, FORCEMEAT IS not a weapon from *Game of Thrones*. There are several kinds of forcemeats, but for this scenario think sausage. When fat and protein are bound together by an emulsion, they cook differently. Forcemeats aren't bad, but when it comes to a burger, they are far from desirable. So don't throw your beef back and forth like a softball because the friction and warmth from your hands will begin to melt the fat and you will start to form a lousy, unintentional burger travesty.

Your patties' dimensions are carved in stone. We can only guarantee a righteous burger if you trust us here.

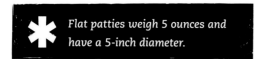
Flat patties weigh 5 ounces and have a 5-inch diameter.

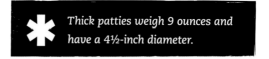
Thick patties weigh 9 ounces and have a 4½-inch diameter.

Patty presses can help you to create uniform burgers without over-handling them. We like the 4½-inch Weston Hamburger Press and the 5-inch Miss Beefy Burger Maker, both readily available online and in kitchen supply stores. When pressing your burger, apply just enough force to create a uniform thickness with a round, smooth edge. Place the formed patties on a baking sheet lined with parchment. Chill in the fridge until ready to cook.

You've chosen your beef thoughtfully, it's freshly ground, you've added wet seasonings if you're using them, and the patties have been formed and chilled. *But remember*, you haven't seasoned your patties with salt or a dry rub because you haven't started cooking...*yet.*

SEASONING

In the professional cooking world, seasoning meat means one thing: a liberal dusting of kosher salt and freshly cracked black pepper. Kosher salt will give you the cleanest, most neutral flavor; we use kosher salt in all our recipes unless we state otherwise.

Using salt and pepper to season your patties doesn't mean you can't add other layers of flavor. In the following chapter, *Spice the Nation*, we provide an army of seasoning recipes for you to pimp out your burger. If you opt for one of the dry seasonings in this book, you do not need to add additional salt or pepper to the dry seasoning as we've already taken that into account.

However, if you're not using a dry seasoning, season your patties with salt and pepper as follows:

For 5-ounce flat patties use ¼ teaspoon of salt and 5 cracks of black pepper for each side.

For 9-ounce thick patties use ½ teaspoon of salt and 12 cracks of black pepper for each side.

This may sound like a lot of salt, but keep in mind that kosher salt isn't nearly as salty in flavor as iodized, and not all of your seasoning is going to stick to your meat.

No matter what, season meat generously *just* before cooking. Seasoning meat in advance can act like a cure, which is *no bueno*. If salt is in contact with protein for an extended period of time (even just one hour) the salt will draw moisture out of the raw meat.

LET'S COOK

It's almost time to get your pans ready or your grill fired up. But first, we gotta talk heat.

Before you begin the cooking process, make sure the surface of your grill or griddle is at least 400°F (500°F is ideal). Season your meat and gently rub a teaspoon of a cooking fat evenly on the side of the burger that will touch the grill or pan first. By the time you're ready to flip, fat will have started to render out from the top of the burger, ensuring that it will not stick after you've flipped it.

EQUIPMENT IS KEY. Use a stainless steel grilling spatula with a solid 8-inch by 3-inch flipping surface (usually available for around $10). Size matters. You can't afford to leave any bit of brown meat stuck to the grill, or even worse, crack your patty.

While we're at it, invest in a digital instant read thermometer. Checking the temperature of the burger is the single most important element of grilling a burger. A calibrated thermometer never lies. Don't press, don't squeeze; use the thermometer.

GRILL

If you're planning on cooking a thick burger, go outdoors. It takes much longer to cook and needs an extremely hot heat source (500°F is ideal). If you cook it indoors, you'll smoke the living shit out of your house.

When we grill, we never use the cover. Think about it. This turns a grill, which is a direct heat source, into an oven, which is an indirect heat source. If you cover your grill, you'll cook your thick burger too quickly, most likely resulting in an overdone, dried out, crispy puck. Leave the grill top off.

A lot of folks want to know which is better: gas or charcoal? Well, there are pros and cons to both. Gas grills are convenient to start up, but good ones can be pricey. Most folks buy cheap grills with low BTUs, so if you're cooking with gas, just make sure

that the surface of your grill can actually hit 500°F (500°F is ideal).

If you have the time, cooking over charcoal is very rewarding. There is absolutely nothing more satisfying than crumbling up some newspaper, tossing it under a chimney starter filled with natural wood charcoal, and lighting it on fire. Wait until the coals turn grey and ash over, dump that sucker out onto the lower rack, and allow the coals to get it so damn hot you can't keep your hand over it without feeling excruciating discomfort. Charcoal cons? Well, if you've had thirty beers you may burn down the neighborhood.

Did we mention that 500°F is ideal?

FLIPPING 101

We're talking about thick patties here and the timeless debate on flipping. How many times will you flip this 9-ounce burger? Well, maestro, that depends on whom you ask.

> **RICHARD HERE.** I've been a one-time flipper my whole life. I've found that cooking one side, then flipping and cooking the other side has done me well over the years. It's straightforward and the most direct way to get a consistently juicy burger.
>
> If you go this route, use your fingers to make a small indent in the center of each patty before putting them on the grill. This will help you avoid the dreaded softball-shaped burgers most of us are all too familiar with.

1 Once your cooking surface is hot and ready, place your meat on the grill: For a rare burger, grill for 3 minutes per side. For a medium-rare burger, grill for 4 minutes per side, and so on.

2 Before you flip, get your spatula underneath your burger and scrape with precision and force. As you flip, use your other hand to guide and cradle each patty. Yeah, it's hot over that grill. This will only make you tougher.

3 After the flip, continue cooking on the other side until you've reached the desired temperature (see Burger Temp-Timing Chart).

4 If you're topping the patty with cheese, do so before you dismount. Ideally, lay on the cheese when you have 90 seconds left of cooking.

SAMMY'S TURN. I do multiple flips. I'm talking at least flip, flip, flip, flip. This allows for an even convection heat to cook the inside of the burger, give it a dark brown crust on the outside, and maintain a consistent temperature throughout the core. If you want to do multiple flips, prepare to get methodical.

1 Every 2 minutes, carefully flip your burger. After 8 minutes, you should have flipped 3 times, exposing each side to the grill for a total of 4 minutes.

2 Check your burger's temperature. Start temping your burger after the first 8 minutes, and if you're in line with the Burger Temp-Timing chart, you're on track to nail it!

3 Adding cheese? Then do it like you mean it: lay it on the patty 90 seconds before you're done cooking. With our handy Temp-Timing Chart, predicting the final 90 seconds is as easy as staring at a clock.

4 Be sure to do one last temperature check before you remove the burger from the grill. Once you have reached your goal, start drooling in anticipation.

BURGER TEMP-TIMING CHART *on the Grill*

GET IT DONE	INTERIOR TEMPERATURE	AVERAGE COOKING TIME	REMOVE FROM GRILL
RARE	125°F	6-8 minutes	Pull at 125°F
MEDIUM RARE	135°F	8-10 minutes	Pull at 130°F
MEDIUM	140°F	12 minutes	Pull at 135°F
MEDIUM WELL	150°F	14 minutes	Pull at 145°F
WELL	160°F	15 minutes	Pull at 160°F

GRIDDLE

When cooking a flat patty, heat your cast iron over a medium-high flame, either in the kitchen or on the grill. Why cast iron? Well, to properly cook a flat patty, you'll want to ensure you can get a good sear on as much surface area as possible in the five to ten minutes the burger is exposed to the heat source. Cast iron is going to help you get those results. Cooking a burger on a griddle is simple; equipment, technique, and temping rules apply here, too.

1. Make sure your cast iron has been over medium-high heat for 4 to 5 minutes and has been wiped with a very thin coating of either canola or light olive oil to avoid sticking. Don't forget to season that meat!

2. Flat patties require only 1 flip. Get your spatula underneath your burger and scrape with intention. When you flip, use your other hand to guide and cradle each patty. Yeah, yeah, it's hot. We know.

3. Keep an eye on that temperature by checking the temping chart. If you're decorating with sliced cheese, do so when you have 90 seconds left. Once the patty reaches the desired temperature, remove from the griddle and place on a sheet tray with a rack. Time to rest.

BURGER TEMP-TIMING CHART on the Griddle

GET IT DONE	INTERIOR TEMPERATURE	TOTAL COOK TIME	WHEN TO FLIP
RARE	125°F	4 minutes	After 2 minutes
MEDIUM RARE	135°F	5 minutes	After 2½ minutes
MEDIUM	140°F	6 minutes	After 3 minutes
MEDIUM WELL	150°F	8 minutes	After 4 minutes
WELL	160°F	10 minutes	After 5 minutes

RESTING

This rule takes some serious patience, but the results are worth it. Most cooks skip the resting period, and just like that, their burger loses major points. But the science is in: Resting your meat allows for major juice retention, which means more succulence, flavor, and chin-dripping goodness.

Rest your flat patties for 3 minutes and your thick patties for 5 minutes. Keep meat in an environment close to 115°F by loosely wrapping your sheet tray with aluminum foil. It's that simple. And you don't have to stand around like a helpless jackass and drool in anticipation. You can get your bun dressed. Or shotgun a beer.

IF YOU WANT to go the extra step with your burger game, baste your beautiful patty while it cooks with some rendered fat. Pick your fat of choice. Could be beef fat, schmaltz, duck fat, pork fat, lamb fat, anything goes. Just get your favorite pastry brush and spread that melted fat like wildfire onto your patty—and add a whole new level of flavor you might not have thought possible.

2.

SPICE THE NATION

SOUTHWEST MOLE NEGRO / CINCINNATI CHILI BOMB / SOUTHEAST PEPPERCORN RANCH / CALI ASADA / PLYMOUTH ROCK / PORTLANDIA DRY RUB / NOLA SMOKY ANDOUILLE / TEXAS FRITO PIE CRUMBLE / NYC PASTRAMI / DAN'S MEMPHIS RIB RUB

BURGER PURISTS WILL tell you that salt and pepper is all you need to season a patty. While we love the simplicity of beautifully sourced beef with a dusting of salt and pepper, we think there's an opportunity to do even more.

While the composition of our burgers may range from simple to outrageous, the goal always stays the same: to highlight and enhance the natural taste of the meat, not mask it. And since we're never ones to miss an opportunity to add a bit more flavor, we often look to well-crafted blends of seasoning that can serve as the perfect foundation for deliciously seared meat. This extra element will give your burger a stealthy layer of depth and funk that can (and should) lead to mixing and matching components and flavors that you may not have otherwise considered.

You can take your burger in any direction you want based on your own taste buds and style. All that matters is that what your patty is wearing looks good to you. American flavors inspire the recipes in this chapter. Some of these blends may be familiar, others exotic; all will add true grit to your next burger.

There are two types of seasonings here: wet and dry. Keep in mind there is no salt in any of the wet recipes because you can't get that crispy, salty brown crust on your meat if you fold the salt into your ground meat. (Reread the first chapter, *The Meat of the Matter*, if you need a refresher.) If you try to do it both ways (salt *in* your meat and salt *on* your meat), it's going to be *too* salty. So, when choosing a wet seasoning, remember to follow our seasoning recommendations according to the size of the patty you're cooking, and everything will be just fine—and damn tasty, too.

WET SEASONINGS

YIELD: Seasoning for 2 pounds of meat   START TO FINISH: 15 minutes

Season the meat by mixing it with all the ingredients. If grinding your own meat, toss cubed meat with wet seasoning and grind as instructed in the first chapter, *The Meat of the Matter*. If folding the seasoning into store-ground meat, place all ingredients in a large mixing bowl and gently massage into the meat until well incorporated.

Once patties are formed and cooking, remember to season with kosher salt and pepper:

For each 5-ounce flat patty, use ¼ teaspoon of salt and 5 cracks of black pepper for each side.

For each 9-ounce thick patty, use ½ teaspoon of salt and 12 cracks of black pepper for each side.

STORAGE NOTES: *Wet seasonings will keep in your refrigerator for up to three days. Seasoned meat can be refrigerated for one day.*

SOUTHWEST MOLE NEGRO

This recipe uses the distinct flavors of mole negro to transform your burger into a southwestern experience. Abuelas everywhere may curse our names for calling this wet seasoning a mole, but our hearts (and taste buds) are in the right place. For all you gringos out there, we hope you will enjoy these rich and complex Mexican flavors that Americans living in the Southwest have been digging for years.

Scant 1 teaspoon ground cocoa powder

½ teaspoon ground ancho chile

½ teaspoon ground mulato chile

½ teaspoon ground guajillo chile

½ teaspoon ground Mexican cinnamon

½ bunch scallions, thinly sliced

2 garlic cloves, minced

⅔ cup tomatillos, cut into a small dice

Scant 1 teaspoon fresh oregano, roughly chopped

Generous pinch dried thyme

1½ tablespoons peanut butter

1½ tablespoons tomato juice

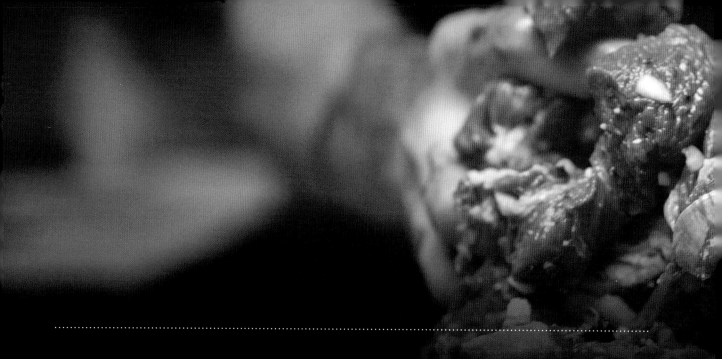

CINCINNATI CHILI BOMB

Cincinnati's chili packs a big umami bomb and rocks a wintery spice profile. It's like mole negro and chili con carne hooked up and had a baby. We've got to hand it to them—folks in the 'Nati are grimy. They put chili on hot dogs and on spaghetti... So why the hell not on a burger?

2½ teaspoons white vinegar

2 tablespoons Steak Sauce (page 146 or store-bought)

2 garlic cloves, minced

½ medium yellow onion, cut into a small dice

1 teaspoon ground cinnamon

Generous pinch ground cloves

Generous pinch ground allspice

½ teaspoon cocoa powder

Scant 1 teaspoon ground cayenne

Scant 1 teaspoon ground cumin

Scant 1 teaspoon black pepper, finely ground

SOUTHEAST PEPPERCORN RANCH

Believe it or not, this simple blend of ingredients is what creates the cherished ranch dressing that Americans love—especially in the South. Those crazy sonsofbitches even dip their pizza in ranch dressing, bless their hearts. Their ranch-infused, buttermilk-pumping hearts.

1½ tablespoons lemon juice

2½ teaspoons red wine vinegar

2½ teaspoons Worcestershire (page 145 or store-bought)

1 teaspoon minced garlic

¾ teaspoon celery seed

1 teaspoon freshly cracked black pepper

CALI ASADA

One of our favorite things about Cali is the warm weather and backyard cookouts. The peeps in Cali know how to do it, and we love getting us some carne asada. It's spicy. Herbaceous. Zesty. Bright. Tangy. And meaty.

½ medium red onion, cut into
a small dice

½ bunch cilantro, roughly chopped

2 garlic cloves, minced

2 tablespoons freshly squeezed lime juice

½ jalapeño, minced

Scant 1 teaspoon freshly cracked
black pepper

½ teaspoon chile de arbol, finely ground

PLYMOUTH ROCK

As Richard will tell you, New Englanders have no problem claiming Thanksgiving as their own personal holiday. They can wake up at ten o'clock like the bums they are, take a road trip to Plymouth Rock, and be home in time for the turkey. It's not just the happiest day of the year for New Englanders; it's a goddamn flavor profile.

1½ tablespoons raspberry vinegar

½ medium white onion, cut into a small dice

8 fresh sage leaves, roughly chopped

2½ teaspoons fresh thyme, roughly chopped

Scant 1 teaspoon fresh rosemary,
roughly chopped

Scant 1 teaspoon white pepper, finely ground

Zest of ½ orange

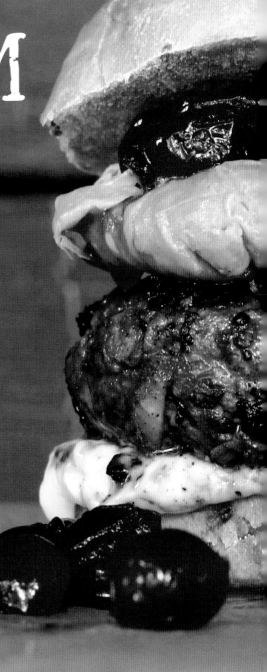

THE
Filthy
PILGRIM
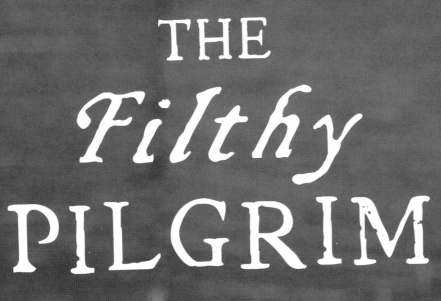

MASHED POTATO & GRAVY ROLL
Page 42

PICKLED CRANBERRIES
Page 195

BUTTERY BAKED ROBIOLA
Page 80

THICK PATTY
SEASONED WITH
PLYMOUTH ROCK Page 25

STANDARD MAYO
Page 133

DRY SEASONINGS

YIELD: Seasoning for 2 pounds of meat   START TO FINISH: 15 minutes

Mix ingredients together and use in place of salt and pepper to season burgers just before cooking. You'll have more than you'll need to season your burgers, but don't fear—the flavors you're blending are so good you're going to want to put them on everything.

STORAGE NOTES: *Tightly sealed, these dry seasonings will keep in your cupboard for up to six months. (If they last that long!)*

PORTLANDIA DRY RUB

If you haven't been to the Pacific Northwest, this recipe is your ticket there. The rich aquaculture and abundance of national forests make this region of America feel like you're entering another world.

Pacific Northwesterners are all about supporting locally and family-owned businesses. We love this mentality, which is why we urge you to get your hands on Jacobsen Sea Salt from Oregon for this recipe. Not only will you get a flavor for this region, you'll taste its ocean, too.

1 ounce dried chanterelles, finely ground

4 tablespoons Jacobsen Sea Salt, crushed into small crystals

10 juniper berries, finely ground

1 ounce freeze-dried apples, crushed with fingers into small crumbs
(if these go in your spice grinder, they will get gummy)

2 tablespoons dark roasted coffee beans, finely ground

NOLA SMOKY ANDOUILLE

There's nothing quite like the smoky spice of Andouille sausage. It's the foundation for and adds depth to some of our most beloved Creole and Cajun dishes. Like all sausages, Andouille's flavor profile is a result of a spice blend and a specific cooking method.

This recipe came about when we started making Andouille from scratch. We had to nail a lot of things to make a badass sausage. Our protein-to-fat ratio had to be on point. The die plates needed to be the perfect size. Our emulsion had to be sticky but not too sticky. The temperature at which we cold smoked needed to be exact. The climate in which we hung our links to age needed to have proper humidity. And most importantly, our spice blend needed to be wicked. Because otherwise we were just making smoked sausages. Not Andouille.

After we conquered all that, we thought... What if we put it on a burger? (Heads up: this blend can be used in any recipe that calls for Cajun spice.)

2 tablespoons smoked salt

1 tablespoon black pepper, finely ground

1 tablespoon white peppercorn, finely ground

2 tablespoons smoked paprika

2 teaspoons ground chipotle

1 tablespoon dry mustard powder

1 teaspoon onion powder

1 teaspoon granulated garlic

1 teaspoon dried thyme

1 tablespoon dried marjoram

1 teaspoon ground allspice

12 cloves, finely ground

TEXAS FRITO PIE CRUMBLE

Fact. This crumble is neither a wet seasoning nor a dry seasoning. Fact. This crumble hits your burger after the patty is cooked. Fact. There's no integrity involved with this recipe.

10½ ounces FRITOS Chili Cheese Flavored Corn Chips, finely ground in food processor

1 cheese powder packet from a box of your favorite mac and cheese

1 guacamole seasoning packet

1 tablespoon chili powder

Mix together and sprinkle directly onto your burger during the resting phase.

When applying this crumble, listen to your heart and don't hold back.

NYC PASTRAMI

We really like pastrami.

- ¼ cup black pepper, coarsely ground
- 1 tablespoon yellow mustard seed, coarsely ground
- 1 tablespoon whole coriander, coarsely ground
- 1 tablespoon brown sugar
- 1 tablespoon kosher salt

DAN'S MEMPHIS RIB RUB

It's been said that no city does ribs better than Memphis. You can get 'em wet or dry, and they come baby back or sparerib. We're sparerib lovers and prefer 'em dry. If you ever find yourself preparing dry spareribs in Memphis, make sure you stick to the code. First and foremost, source quality meat. Second, practice proper butchery. Last, think about the rub. Everyone thinks theirs is the best.

This is our version—an exquisitely balanced all-purpose rib rub. It was perfected and passed on to us from a great friend and fellow chef, Dan Crothers. It's damn good on pork, works wonders for chicken, and even stands up to the bold flavor of beef! Next time you wanna add a lil' Memphis to your burger, give this rub a try.

- 1 cup light brown sugar
- 6 tablespoons kosher salt
- 1 tablespoon chili powder
- 1 teaspoon cayenne
- 1 teaspoon freshly cracked black pepper
- 1 teaspoon onion powder
- 1 teaspoon garlic powder
- 1 teaspoon dried thyme
- 1 teaspoon Old Bay seasoning

AND NOW A BRIEF PASTRAMI INTERLUDE

I spent the entire summer of 2011 obsessively researching the craft of making pastrami, with the ambitious desire to develop my own unique preparation of the decadent delicatessen delight. Upon submerging myself into the vast, fascinating world of pastrami, I discovered that if I were going to succeed at making this succulent hunk of meat, I would need to develop my own signature spice rub. At first, I didn't know what to do, mainly because the possibilities seemed endless. What style did I want to emulate? Romanian, Turkish, Jewish, Montrealais?

The countless options distracted my focus and my direction was lost; at one point, I was experimenting with a spice rub that had twenty-two ingredients. I was out of control and needed an intervention. I slapped myself silly with sandwich-sliced Swiss, took a shot of Russian dressing, and looked myself dead in the mirror. "What do you really want to taste?" I asked myself.

Knowing damn well that failure was not an option, I rose to the challenge, the way a well-proofed loaf of marble rye rises while in the oven. First, I worked through the technicalities. As with most decent crusts or rubs, I would need salt and sugar. (Light brown sugar is how I roll.) Then I thought, well, I have to use black pepper, mustard seed, and coriander. Remembering the complicated blunders of my previous attempts, I stopped myself there. My first attempt at rationing out each ingredient was a success, and after only an hour of cooking, the aroma was so heavenly that I knew this was something special. **– SAMMY**

Ah, pastrami, where do I begin? I am not a religious person, but traditions (ahem, food) are truly near and dear to my heart when it comes to my Jewish background. I was raised with a healthy dose of latkes, matzo balls, and schmaltz, and my Polish roots only complemented the matter with the obvious crossover of caraway and pierogi. I also have a lot of family in Montreal, so when I was a kid, my family would always load up the van and head to our great neighbors to the north, where we heartily filled our bellies with smoked meat from Schwartz's, crackly and warm sesame bagels with a good schmear of cream cheese, and way too many desserts to count (I can thank my mom, aunt, and grandmother for that last one).

Pastrami, specifically, has a unique hold on me. Back in 2012, my then girlfriend Katie and I were in New York City for our annual food "research" trip, during which we planned a visit to the infamous Katz's Deli. Thanks to Meg Ryan and what is unequivocally our favorite meal on the planet, that massive pastrami on rye with mustard has forever since held a special place in our hearts. Fast forward to less than a year later. With a special shipment of Katz's pastrami, rye bread, and some uncomfortably large pickles, I proposed to Katie on top of a hill on the outskirts of Boston. I'll never forget how gorgeous the ring looked on Katie's finger as she held the rye in her hands. That sandwich, and pastrami in general, will instantly take me back to all of those moments in the most special way possible. **– RICHARD**

3.

YEASTY BOYS

IPA SESAME SEED BUNS / BACON, SCALLION & CREAM CHEESE ENGLISH MUFFINS / MASHED POTATO & GRAVY ROLLS / GLUTEN-FREE MASHED POTATO ROLLS / PIZZA STROMBOLI BUNS / ASTRID'S PALEO WAFFLES / LOWCOUNTRY CORNBREAD / GORDITAS / STUFFED PRETZEL BUNS / BEEF & ROSEMARY BISCUITS / ULTIMATE JEW*ISH* RYE BREAD / BALLAH' / GLAZED DONUTS WITH FOIE-STING

BREAD HAS THE power to make or break any great sandwich, and the burger is certainly no exception. When it comes to burger buns, nothing is off limits. From the humble potato bun to the far-fetched waffle to the freshly made donut, the only rule is that the bun must fit the patty like a glove. There are few things worse in burgerland than a poor meat-to-bun ratio. Many burgers miss the mark when a lovely patty is sandwiched between a towering bun that completely overwhelms it. The focus should be the meat; the bun is merely there to support and complement the patty (and to tell the burger it doesn't look fat every now and then).

If you're dead set against baking your own buns and there is nothing we can do to convince you otherwise then we want you to know we're okay with that (it's not like we're banging out buns every day, after all). But if you're going to purchase your burger bread, remember that the bun isn't a mere afterthought. It provides your burger with structural integrity and plays a primary role in your burger's overall flavor.

Whether it is a pack of classic sesame seed buns, Martin's potato rolls, or a slowrise sourdough, just do us one favor: pick your buns with purpose. With conviction. Thoughtfully. Go with something fresh; your local bakery is a great starting point, and there are tremendous hand-crafted baked goods out there to fulfill all of your burger needs.

But if you're willing to rise to the occasion, then read on, comrade, because we're going to get down and dirty with some flour and yeast.

More and more great chefs serve their burgers on house-made buns, elevating the meal and wowing their patrons. (Don't let the house-made part throw you; you're just as good as those guys.) If you're ready to throw some buns in the oven, you'll find the process immensely rewarding and far simpler than you may think. These recipes take time, but they're surprisingly very little work. With a bit of advanced planning, you could easily whip up a batch of hot buns while hanging with your peeps. If you're not familiar with the nooks and crannies of baking, read each recipe several times, put your head down, and focus. You may never go back to store-bought buns again.

With all of our bun recipes, we give you a wide range for the amount of flour you'll need. True bread-making nerds (you know who you are) will tell you that using a scale to measure by weight is the only way to go. Sure, measuring by weight is far more accurate than measuring by volume, but so many other factors are at play, including but not limited to: temperature, humidity, and altitude.

The trick to making bread isn't finding that exact amount of flour; it's in keeping an eye on your dough. If the dough is so sticky that it feels like a gooey mess, it's too wet. Add flour in ¼-cup increments until you get the right consistency. Your dough should feel tacky, not wet. Once you find the right balance, you'll get the feel of it in no time.

FOR THOSE WHO want to do it like grandma or just don't have a stand mixer, you can make all the buns in this chapter the old world way. Simply follow the instructions the same way, using a large mixing bowl, some elbow grease while kneading, and a winning attitude. You can do it, you yeasty beast, you.

YOU CAN DO IT!

TO TOAST OR NOT TO TOAST?

Believe it or not, this is a hot-button issue in the burger world.

Toasting adds texture, but some prefer the cold, submissive untoasted bun. We like it somewhere in the middle (warm but not too crispy), which creates that lovely balance of structured fluffiness. In a perfect world, once your burger comes off the grill or griddle to rest, your cut buns get toasted right on those grates or in that pan, soaking up all the extra beef drippings.

IPA SESAME SEED BUNS

YIELD: 8 to 12 buns   START TO FINISH: 2½ to 3 hours   ACTIVE TIME: About 45 minutes

This is our version of the classic hamburger bun. To amplify that textbook yeastiness and airiness, we add quality beer and milk. We took that ho-hum bun from our earliest burger memories and raised the bar.

2½ teaspoons active dry yeast

2 teaspoons granulated sugar

⅓ cup warm water (100-110°F)

4 ounces IPA beer, preferably Harpoon IPA

3 eggs (1 beaten with a fork in a small bowl, reserved)

1½ teaspoons kosher salt

4 tablespoons unsalted butter, melted

½ cup milk (any will do, buttermilk, whole milk, etc.)

3½ to 5 cups all-purpose flour

1 tablespoon olive oil

¼ cup sesame seeds

1. Combine yeast, sugar, and water in a small bowl. Stir gently and allow the yeast to activate, about 5 minutes. You'll know it's ready when the yeast is foamy.

2. In a stand mixer with the dough hook attachment, add the yeast mixture, beer, 2 eggs, salt, and melted butter. Mix on low for 1 to 2 minutes. Add the milk and mix to combine.

3. Begin adding the flour 1 cup at a time, mixing on low to incorporate. Once you've added 3 cups of flour, increase the speed to medium-low and let the machine run for a minute.

4. Stop the machine and touch the dough. If it is very sticky and wet, add more flour, ¼ cup at a time, and continue mixing for another minute. Continue in this fashion. Once the dough no longer feels wet, mix on medium until it is smooth and shiny, about 3 to 5 minutes.

5. Lightly brush a large mixing bowl with olive oil. Add the dough to the bowl and turn to coat. Cover with a towel or plastic wrap and let it rise in a warm spot until doubled in size, about 1 hour. Meanwhile, preheat the oven to 400°F.

6. Once dough has doubled in size, turn out onto a large, lightly floured surface, and divide into 12 pieces for smaller burgers or 8 pieces for larger burgers. Cover with a clean towel.

7 Working with 1 piece at a time (and keeping the remaining pieces covered until ready to use), shape the dough into discs. Place the discs onto a large baking sheet lined with parchment paper and repeat with the remaining dough. Don't crowd the buns on the baking sheet; use multiple baking sheets if necessary.

8 Cover the buns and place them in a warm spot (right by the preheated oven will do the trick). Allow them to proof and rise a second time until doubled in size, about 15 to 20 minutes.

9 Brush each piece of dough with the beaten egg and sprinkle sesame seeds on top. Bake in the oven for about 10 to 12 minutes if making smaller buns (14 to 16 minutes if making larger buns), rotating the pan halfway through, until buns are golden brown and internal temperature has reached 200°F on an instant read thermometer.

10 Cool slightly before slicing in half.

STORAGE NOTES: *Tightly wrapped buns will keep at room temperature for two to three days. They also freeze well.*

TASTY WITH:

Smoked Heirlooms, Watercress, Chive & Cream Cheese Spread, Peameal Bacon

BACON, SCALLION & CREAM CHEESE ENGLISH MUFFINS

YIELD: 12 English muffins   START TO FINISH: 2 to 3 hours   ACTIVE TIME: About 45 minutes to 1 hour

Nowadays, burger shops flock to the nooks and crannies of an English muffin, which—when you think about it—is the perfect shape for a hamburger patty.

Commercial English muffins are too thin to withstand the onslaught of juice that's sure to come your way, though. Our muffins are bigger, thicker, and begin their cooking process in a hefty cast iron skillet, which slowly develops all those pockets of pleasure. Playing on the breakfast theme, we incorporate cream cheese, bacon, and scallions into the dough, creating a sweet-and-savory balancing act that would be ideal with or without a burger. But who are we kidding, this is a burger book, so lay it on there!

2½ teaspoons active dry yeast

2 teaspoons plus ¼ cup granulated sugar, divided

⅓ cup warm water (100-110°F)

1 cup buttermilk

2 teaspoons kosher salt

2 tablespoons unsalted butter, cubed and softened

3 tablespoons cream cheese, softened

8 bacon slices, cooked, cooled, roughly chopped, and divided

½ bunch scallions, thinly sliced (can substitute freshly chopped chives)

3½ to 5 cups all-purpose flour

1 tablespoon olive oil

¼ cup cornmeal for dusting, or as needed

1 egg, beaten with a fork

1   Combine yeast, 2 teaspoons sugar, and water in a small bowl. Stir gently and allow the yeast to activate, about 5 minutes. You'll know it's ready when the yeast is foamy.

2   In a stand mixer with the dough hook attachment, add the yeast mixture, buttermilk, remaining ¼ cup sugar, and salt. Combine on low to incorporate. Add the butter, cream cheese, half of the bacon, and all of the scallions. Mix to combine.

3   Begin adding the flour, 1 cup at a time, and mix on low to incorporate. Once you've added 3 cups of flour, increase the speed to medium-low and let the machine run for a minute.

4   Stop the machine and touch the dough. If it is very sticky and wet, add more flour, ¼ cup at a time, and continue mixing for another minute. Continue in this fashion. Once the dough no longer feels wet, mix on medium until it is smooth and shiny, about 3 to 5 minutes.

5   Lightly brush a large mixing bowl with olive oil. Add the dough to the bowl and turn to coat. Cover with a towel or plastic wrap and let it rise in a warm spot until doubled in size, about 1 hour. Meanwhile, preheat the oven to 400°F.

6   Once dough has doubled in size, lightly coat a large baking sheet with cornmeal. Divide into 12 balls. Working with 1

dough ball at a time, take each ball and slightly flatten. Carefully roll it in some of the cornmeal. Repeat with the remaining balls of dough, using a second baking sheet if necessary. Keep the shaped dough rounds covered with a towel as you work.

7 Place a large cast iron skillet over medium-low heat and allow it to heat up, about 2 to 3 minutes. Add 2 tablespoons of cornmeal to the skillet and add as many rounds as will comfortably fit without overcrowding (they will expand in the pan as they cook), keeping the remaining muffins covered with a towel. Cook the English muffins, lowering the heat to ensure the cornmeal doesn't burn, until they start to turn golden brown, about 10 to 12 minutes on each side. You want to go slowly here and really allow those pockets to develop.

8 After all of the English muffins have browned, brush each with the beaten egg. Sprinkle them with the remaining bacon (you did remember to save that bacon and not eat it, right?) and bake until they are a golden brown and internal temperature has reached 200°F on an instant read thermometer, about 12 to 15 minutes.

9 Let the muffins cool slightly. Using the tines of a fork, poke holes around the circumference of each muffin and then pry them open.

10 These bad boys are ready to be topped with your favorite burger right out of the oven. Once cooled, they can be toasted and buttered before getting acquainted with the patty.

STORAGE NOTES: *Tightly wrapped muffins will keep in the refrigerator for several days. Reheat in a toaster before eating.*

TASTY WITH:
Bloody Mary Ketchup,
Peameal Bacon, Jammy Yolks

MASHED POTATO & GRAVY ROLLS

YIELD: 8 to 12 rolls   START TO FINISH: 2 to 3 hours   ACTIVE TIME: 30 to 45 minutes

Potato rolls are about as classic as you can get. We are fond of the soft, squishy Martin's potato rolls (great in a pinch), but we think these are even better.

Strangely, homemade potato rolls rarely use actual potato, so we upped the ante and went with a loaded potato approach, folding in sour cream and chive mashed potatoes and gravy, then sprinkling in potato flakes for even more oomph. (Of course, your leftover mashed potatoes work just as well.) Follow the variation to make these guys gluten free!

MASHED POTATOES

2 medium Yukon Gold potatoes, skin on and cut into 1-inch pieces

½ cup sour cream

1 tablespoon freshly chopped chives

Generous pinch kosher salt

MASHED POTATO & GRAVY ROLLS

2½ teaspoons active dry yeast

Pinch granulated sugar

½ cup reserved potato water or warm water (100-110°F)

1 teaspoon kosher salt

2 cups mashed potatoes (use leftovers if you have them)

3 eggs (1 beaten with a fork in a small bowl, reserved)

1 package instant gravy (yup, we went there)

4 to 5 cups all-purpose flour

1 cup potato starch or potato flour (available in grocery stores)

¼ cup potato flakes

1. Add potatoes to a pot of cold water. (Water should cover potatoes by 1 inch.) Bring to a gentle boil, reduce to a simmer, and cook until the potatoes are soft, about 12 minutes.

2. Drain the potatoes; reserve the water and set aside. Return the potatoes to the empty pot and mash. Add sour cream, chives, and salt. Taste for seasoning and set aside.

3. Combine the yeast, sugar, and water in a small bowl. Stir gently and allow the yeast to activate, about 5 minutes. You'll know it's ready when the yeast is foamy.

4. In a stand mixer with the dough hook attachment, add the yeast mixture, salt, and mashed potatoes. Mix on low to incorporate.

5. Add 2 eggs and mix to combine.

6. In a small bowl, add instant gravy, 4 cups of flour, potato starch, and potato flakes. Whisk to combine, then add to yeast mixture. Mix on low until ingredients are evenly incorporated and just binding together, about 2 to 3 minutes.

7. Increase speed to medium and mix until the dough comes together into a ball, about 1 minute.

8. Stop the machine and touch the dough. If it is very sticky and wet, add more flour, ¼ cup at a time, and continue mixing for another minute. Continue in this fashion. Once the dough no longer feels wet, mix on medium until it is smooth and shiny, about 3 to 5 minutes.

9 Lightly brush a large mixing bowl with olive oil. Add the dough to the bowl and turn to coat. Cover the dough and let it rise in a warm spot until doubled in size, about 1 hour.

10 Preheat the oven to 400°F.

11 Once dough has doubled in size, turn out onto a large, lightly floured surface. Divide into 12 pieces for smaller burgers or 8 pieces for larger burgers. Cover with a clean towel.

12 Working with 1 piece at a time (and keeping the remaining pieces covered until ready to use), shape the dough into discs. Place the discs onto a large baking sheet lined with parchment paper and repeat with the remaining dough. Don't crowd the rolls on the baking sheet; use multiple baking sheets if necessary.

13 Cover the rolls and place them in a warm spot (right by the preheated oven will do the trick). Allow them to proof and rise a second time until doubled in size, about 15 to 20 minutes.

14 Brush each piece of dough with the beaten egg. Bake in the oven for about 10 to 12 minutes if making smaller buns (14 to 16 minutes if making larger buns), rotating the pan halfway through, until rolls are golden brown and internal temperature has reached 200°F on an instant read thermometer.

15 Cool slightly before slicing in half.

STORAGE NOTES: *Tightly wrapped rolls will keep at room temperature for two to three days. They also freeze well.*

TASTY WITH:

Plymouth Rock, Buttery Baked Robiola, Standard Mayo, Pickled Cranberries

··

We call this the Filthy Pilgrim SEE PAGE 26

GLUTEN-FREE VERSION

Because gluten-free folks deserve a great roll, too.

Simply nix the all-purpose flour, potato starch (or potato flour), potato flakes, and the instant gravy. Instead of the all-purpose flour, substitute 2½ cups all-purpose gluten-free flour (such as King Arthur or Bob's Red Mill), or more as needed.

Follow the recipe until the last step. Then brush each piece of dough with the beaten egg and sprinkle with ¼ cup cheese. Bake in the oven as instructed above.

PIZZA STROMBOLI BUNS

YIELD: 8 to 12 buns   START TO FINISH: 2 to 3 hours   ACTIVE TIME: About 45 minutes

Sometimes you want a pizza *and* a burger. What do you do? Make pizza buns!

  Inspired by stromboli, these pizza buns are just that: a fairly straightforward pizza dough that is rolled with pepperoni and mozzarella, shaped into buns, then quickly baked to make the ultimate pizza-meets-bun experience.

2½ teaspoons active dry yeast

2 teaspoons granulated sugar

⅓ cup warm water (100-110°F), plus 1¼ cups room temperature water

1½ teaspoons kosher salt

4 to 5 cups "00" flour (you can use all-purpose flour, but "00" is the best!)

3 tablespoons olive oil, divided

⅓ pound sliced pepperoni, cut into strips

¾ cup shredded mozzarella

1 egg, beaten with a fork

1 Combine yeast, sugar, and ⅓ cup warm water in a small bowl. Stir gently and allow the yeast to activate, about 5 minutes. You'll know it's ready when the yeast is foamy.

2 In a stand mixer with the dough hook attachment, add the yeast mixture and salt and combine on low to incorporate. Add the remaining water, flour, and 2 tablespoons of olive oil and mix on low until it starts to come together, about 1 minute.

3 Increase the speed to medium and mix until the dough comes together fully and pulls away from the sides and bottom of the bowl. Stop the machine and touch the dough. If it is very sticky and wet, add more flour, ¼ cup at a time, and continue mixing for another minute. Continue in this fashion. Once the dough no longer feels wet, mix on medium until it is smooth and shiny, about 3 to 5 minutes.

4 Lightly brush a large bowl with remaining olive oil. Add the dough and turn to coat. Cover with a towel or plastic wrap and let it rise in a warm spot until doubled in size, about 1 hour. Meanwhile, preheat the oven to 400°F.

5 Once dough has doubled in size, turn out onto a large, lightly floured surface. Divide into 12 pieces for smaller burgers or 8 pieces for larger burgers. Take a small amount of pepperoni and mozzarella (about 2 tablespoons of each) and fold them into the dough until well incorporated. Flatten into rounds, shaping all the rounds of dough in this manner.

6 Brush each bun with the beaten egg. Bake until golden brown and internal temperature has reached 200°F on an instant read thermometer, about 10 to 12 minutes if making smaller rolls (14 to 16 minutes if making larger rolls).

7 Cool slightly, slice in half, and enjoy with your favorite burger.

STORAGE NOTES: *Buns can be stored in the refrigerator for several days or in the freezer for several weeks.*

TASTY WITH:
King Frico, Standard Mayo, Pepperoncini Cubanelles

ASTRID'S PALEO WAFFLES

YIELD: 4 waffles (2 buns)   START TO FINISH: 15 to 20 minutes

When Sammy actually wakes up before noon, his wife Astrid sometimes surprises him with a stacked plate of chow. As a nutritionist and fitness professional, Astrid developed this particular recipe to fall in line with the Paleo diet—a grain- and legume-free way of eating that is modeled after the patterns of our Paleolithic-era predecessors. Sandwich your burger between these waffles and load it up, caveman-style.

   This recipe is easily doubled if you are feeding more than just you and your overnight guest (wink wink).

1 cup almond flour

1½ teaspoons baking powder

2 tablespoons psyllium husk (available online or at specialty food stores)

2 tablespoons coconut flour

½ teaspoon kosher salt

3 eggs

½ cup unsweetened almond milk

2 tablespoons melted butter, plus more for greasing

¼ cup honey

SPECIAL EQUIPMENT:

Waffle iron

TASTY WITH:

Gooey Jucy Lucy,
Jalapeño Hot Sauce,
Smoked Tasso Ham

1 Preheat waffle iron.

2 In a medium bowl, whisk together all dry ingredients.

3 Mix in eggs, milk, 2 tablespoons of butter, and honey. Whisk until smooth. Let rest for 5 minutes.

4 Whisk until smooth again. (You'll notice the batter is thicker. That's because the psyllium has had time to gel and provide structure to the batter in place of gluten.)

5 Grease waffle iron with remaining butter. Pour batter equally to yield 4 waffles. Cook until golden brown and slightly crispy, about 3 to 4 minutes.

6 Each waffle is meant to be half of your bun, so 2 waffles per burger. Load it up with your favorite breakfast goodies and get your day going right!

STORAGE NOTES: *Waffles will keep in the refrigerator for one to two days. Reheat in toaster if not eating right off the iron.*

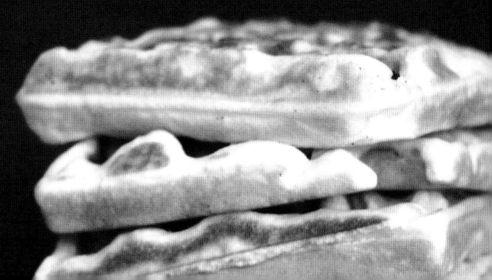

LOWCOUNTRY CORNBREAD

YIELD: 7 muffins   START TO FINISH: 1 hour   ACTIVE TIME: 15 minutes

We love and respect the authenticity and heritage of cornbread all over America, but we think the folks in America's Lowcountry have perfected it. Before pouring their batter into a cast iron pan, they heat the pan over medium heat, add grease (in the South, that's the textbook term for lard), pour in the batter, and jump start the browning process on the stove before the muffins go into the oven. This bonus step allows for a far sturdier crust to form along the bottom of your cornbread. That nice chew and crispiness will give your muffins enough structure to morph into a badass burger bun.

1 cup all-purpose flour

1 cup corn flour

1 teaspoon kosher salt

¾ cup granulated sugar

1 tablespoon baking powder

¼ pound unsalted butter,
    melted and cooled slightly

2 eggs

2 cups buttermilk

¼ cup light olive oil or canola oil

¼ cup lard or bacon fat

SPECIAL EQUIPMENT:

Cast iron muffin or drop biscuit
    pan (3¼- to 3½-inch
    diameter cups)

1 Preheat the oven to 400°F.

2 In a large bowl, whisk together flour, corn flour, salt, sugar, and baking powder.

3 Add the butter, eggs, buttermilk, and oil and whisk vigorously until smooth.

4 Heat cast iron muffin pan over medium-low heat. Place about 1 teaspoon of fat in each slot. (Butter will work in a pinch.)

5 Spoon in cornbread batter, filling each cavity ¾ full, and allow bottoms to brown for 2 minutes.

6 Place muffin pan in oven and bake until muffins are fully set, about 20 to 25 minutes. Muffins are done when an inserted toothpick comes out clean.

7 Allow muffins to cool for 15 minutes before handling. Cut in half horizontally to resemble a burger bun, add your patty, load it up with your favorite fixings, and get your grub on.

STORAGE NOTES: *Cornbread will keep for several days but works best as a burger bun when freshly baked.*

TASTY WITH:

Southeast Peppercorn Ranch, Pimento EZ CHZ, Pan Fried Pickled Green Tomatoes, Chicken Fried Pork Belly

MASA HARINA is a corn flour made from cooked hominy, which is used to make tortillas, tamales, empanadas, pupusas, arepas, and, you guessed it, gorditas. You can find masa harina in the Latin aisle of most grocery stores, usually in a bright orange bag. Specialty stores will often carry it in the baking/grains aisle. There is no substitution for masa and it's a multitasking ingredient, so grab a bag!

GORDITAS

YIELD: 6 gorditas (3 buns)   START TO FINISH: 30 minutes

Gordita literally translates into "little fat girl." Gorditas are traditionally two to three inches in diameter, fried, and stuffed. But we're Americans, so we're making them bigger. And instead of stuffing your burger inside one of these gorditas, we suggest you make two of them for every burger you're preparing. Because, dammit, you deserve it.

Double this recipe and pan fry in batches if you're feeding a crowd.

1½ cups masa harina

½ cup all-purpose flour

¾ teaspoon baking powder

1 teaspoon kosher salt, plus more for seasoning

2 tablespoons lard or bacon fat, plus ¼ cup for pan frying

1 cup hot water

TASTY WITH:

Cali Asada, Salsa Quemada, Quick Pickled Red Onions, Creamy Chimichurri, Camotes al Horno Crema —*and some Monterey Jack cheese and sliced avocado, because it's so damn good.*

SEE NEXT PAGE →

1️⃣ In a large bowl, mix all dry ingredients together.

2️⃣ Add lard (or bacon fat) to dry ingredients. Incorporate water 1 tablespoon at a time. Mixture should be dry enough to form and press, but wet enough so it doesn't crumble apart. Continue to add water in this fashion until you reach the "Goldilocks" zone, where everything is just right. You might need a little less than 1 cup of water; you might need a little bit more.

3️⃣ Portion dough into balls using a ⅓-cup measuring cup.

4️⃣ Using the bottom of a pot or a press, press each ball flat until it's about ¼-inch thick with a 5-inch diameter.

5️⃣ Heat cast iron pan or griddle over medium heat. Lube cast iron with lard or bacon fat and fry gorditas until golden brown on each side, about 2 to 3 minutes per side.

6️⃣ Place gorditas on a brown paper bag and season with salt on both sides while still warm. Rest until cool enough to handle.

7️⃣ Each gordita is half of your bun, so place a gordita on your plate, load it up with your burger and goodies of choice, slap another gordita on top, and booyah, you're in for a south-of-the-border treat.

STORAGE NOTES: *These gorditas eat best when right out of the pan. Uncooked dough will keep in the refrigerator for up to one week.*

THE
WALKER

TEXAS RANGER

MONTEREY JACK CHEESE

STACK of **PATTIES**
SEASONED WITH
CALI ASADA

Page 25

GORDITAS
Page 49

QUICK PICKLED RED ONIONS

Page 110

AVOCADO SLICES

CAMOTES AL HORNO CREMA

Page 160

STUFFED PRETZEL BUNS

YIELD: 12 buns   START TO FINISH: 2 to 3 hours   ACTIVE TIME: About 45 minutes

We fully support the pretzel bun trend, but these buns go a little further. They're mixed with ketchup, mustard, and cheese, stuffed with more cheese and capicola, then boiled and baked to get that beautiful pretzel sheen. One note: chill them before cutting them in half to make sure the cheese stays in place. It'll be worth the wait, we promise.

2½ teaspoons active dry yeast

2 teaspoons granulated sugar

⅓ cup warm water (100-110°F)

4 ounces beer, preferably IPA (we use Harpoon)

3 eggs (1 beaten with a fork in a small bowl, reserved)

1½ teaspoons kosher salt

4 tablespoons unsalted butter, melted and slightly cooled

½ cup milk (any will do: buttermilk, whole milk, etc.)

¼ cup Umami Ketchup (page 119 or Heinz)

¼ cup "Burn Your Nose Hairs" Yellow Mustard (page 128 to store-bought)

½ cup shredded cheddar cheese, divided into two ¼ cup piles

3½ to 5 cups all-purpose flour

1 tablespoon olive oil

8 slices hot or mild capicola, cut into thin strips

¼ cup baking soda

1 Combine yeast, sugar, and warm water in a small bowl. Stir gently and allow the yeast to activate, about 5 minutes. You'll know it's ready when the yeast is foamy.

2 In a stand mixer with the dough hook attachment, add the yeast mixture, beer, 2 eggs, salt, and melted butter. Mix on low for no more than 2 minutes. Add the milk and mix to combine. Add the ketchup, mustard, and ¼ cup cheese. Mix to combine.

3 Begin adding the flour (you may not need all of it) 1 cup at a time, gently mixing on low to incorporate.

4 Once you've added 3 cups of flour, increase the speed to medium-low and let the machine run for a minute. Stop the machine and touch the dough. If it is sticky and wet, add ¼ cup of flour at a time until the dough is tacky but not wet to the touch.

5 Once the dough reaches desired consistency, mix on medium for about 3 to 5 minutes until it is smooth and shiny.

6 Lightly brush a large mixing bowl with olive oil. Add the dough to the bowl and turn to coat. Cover with a towel or plastic wrap and let it rise in a warm spot until doubled in size, about 1 hour.

7 Preheat the oven to 425°F.

8 On a large cutting board, divide the dough into 12 pieces. Working with 1 piece at a time (and keeping the remaining pieces covered until ready to use), take a small handful of the remaining cheese and capicola and add a little to each piece of dough, folding it over onto itself until no cheese or capicola is visible.

9 Roll out each piece of dough into a long rope, about 7 to 8 inches each. Make a U-shape with the rope, cross the ends over

each other to make an X, and press into the bottom to form a pretzel shape. The shape should be tight. Take care not to leave large holes or spaces. We're making pretzel buns, not your average pretzels. Slightly flatten and pinch together if necessary.

10 Place the shaped pretzel buns onto a large baking sheet lined with parchment paper and repeat with the remaining dough. Don't crowd the buns on the baking sheet (use multiple baking sheets if necessary) and make sure to cover them with a clean towel as you work.

11 Allow the shaped pretzel buns to proof and rise for a second time, covered with a towel in a warm spot (right by the preheated oven would do the trick) until doubled in size, about 15 to 20 minutes.

12 While the dough is resting, bring a large pot half full of water to a boil. Once the water is boiling and the dough has completed the second rise, add the baking soda to the water. (It will bubble up!)

13 Add a few pretzels at a time to the water, boiling for about 1 minute on each side. Using a slotted spoon, remove and place on a clean baking sheet. Boil the remaining shaped dough. Cool slightly.

14 Brush each boiled pretzel bun with the beaten egg and bake in the oven, rotating the pan halfway through, until pretzel buns are golden brown and the interior temperature has reached 200°F on an instant read thermometer, about 15 to 20 minutes.

15 Cool completely before slicing in half.

STORAGE NOTES: *Buns can be stored in the refrigerator for up to a week or in the freezer for several weeks.*

TASTY WITH:
$30 Fondue, Bacon & Beer Honey Mustard

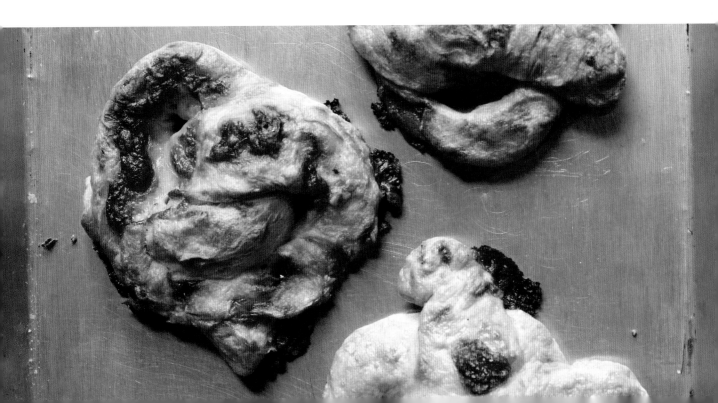

BEEF & ROSEMARY BISCUITS

YIELD: 6 biscuits   START TO FINISH: About 6 hours   ACTIVE TIME: 1½ hours

Let's face it; most biscuits are dry, too sweet, and boring. We yearned for a far more savory biscuit, one that had elements that would pair with a burger without getting too complicated.

To amplify the beefiness, we swapped out cubed butter with cubed rendered beef fat and a dusting of fresh rosemary. And because these biscuits use both yeast and baking powder as leavening agents, they are guaranteed to be soft and fluffy yet hearty enough for your burger. Biscuits are best warm from the oven, so get those burgers ready while you bake. Simply slice each biscuit in half and use in place of a humdrum bun.

8 tablespoons beef fat (available at most grocery stores), divided

2½ teaspoons active dry yeast

2 teaspoons granulated sugar

1 cup warm buttermilk (100-110°F)

2 tablespoons fresh rosemary, finely chopped, divided

2 teaspoons kosher salt, divided

1 teaspoon baking soda

1 teaspoon baking powder

2 cups all-purpose flour

1 Place 8 tablespoons of beef fat in a medium saucepan and turn the heat to medium-low. The fat will begin to render and melt. Turn heat to low (adding a drop or 2 of water to help get the fat going) and cook until the fat has completely rendered, 30-45 minutes. Pass through a fine-mesh sieve to catch any leftover solids. Chill in a clean bowl until firm, about 2 to 3 hours, or until ready to use.

2 Combine yeast, sugar, and warm buttermilk in a small bowl. Stir gently and allow the yeast to activate, about 5 minutes. You'll know it's ready when the yeast is foamy.

3 In a large bowl, combine 1½ tablespoons rosemary, 1 teaspoon salt, baking soda, baking powder, and flour. Stir to combine.

4 Working with 1 tablespoon at a time, cut the fat into the flour mixture using your fingers to break it apart and incorporate it until it resembles coarse sand and you've added 6 tablespoons of beef fat. (Reserve the remaining 2 tablespoons of beef fat.)

5 Gently stir in the buttermilk mixture. At first it will look like too much liquid, but continue mixing with your hands to bring the dough together, being careful not to overwork it. It should just barely come together, with a few loose crumbs. Form it into a loose ball, wrap tightly with plastic wrap, and chill until firm, about 1 hour.

TASTY WITH:

Vermont "Velveeta,"
Vidalia Jam,
Dijon

6   Preheat the oven to 425°F.

7   On a cutting board, gently roll out the dough into a disc that's about ½ inch thick. Using a 3½-to 4-inch cookie cutter or drinking glass, cut out 6 rounds of dough, rolling the scraps together once more if necessary. Arrange biscuits on a baking sheet lined with parchment paper.

8   Divide the remaining 2 tablespoons of beef fat among the biscuits, topping each one with a small dollop. Sprinkle the remaining salt and rosemary on the biscuits.

9   Bake until puffy and golden, about 12 to 14 minutes. Cut each biscuit in half and serve warm.

STORAGE NOTES: *Tightly wrapped biscuits will keep at room temperature for one to two days. Reheat them in the toaster before eating.*

ULTIMATE JEW*ISH* RYE BREAD

YIELD: 1 loaf (4-6 buns depending on how thick or thin you slice it)

START TO FINISH: 2½ to 3½ hours   ACTIVE TIME: 30 minutes

We wanted to create the ultimate rye bread for the ultimate deli-inspired burger. Richard, being Jew*ish*, created this recipe to represent all the great delis his parents have carted him to over the years.

To conjure all the famous flavors a good rye is associated with, caraway seeds, mustard, sauerkraut, cornichons, and horseradish are mixed into the dough. After it's sliced and griddled, this rye is the perfect canvas for the ultimate patty melt.

Deli Rye Flavor is available from King Arthur Flour. This ingredient amplifies the flavor but the bread will still be delicious without it.

2½ teaspoons active dry yeast

2 teaspoons granulated sugar

1 cup warm water (100-110°F)

1 teaspoon kosher salt

10 cornichons, chopped, plus ½ cup of their liquid

¼ cup jarred sauerkraut

1½ tablespoons caraway seeds, toasted

¼ cup Dijon (page 128 or store-bought)

1½ teaspoons prepared horseradish

1 teaspoon Deli Rye Flavor

4 to 5 cups all-purpose flour

2 tablespoon olive oil, divided

1 egg, beaten with a fork

1. Combine yeast, sugar, and warm water in a small bowl. Stir gently and allow the yeast to activate, about 5 minutes. You'll know it's ready when the yeast is foamy.

2. In a stand mixer with the dough hook attachment, add the yeast mixture, salt, cornichons and their liquid, sauerkraut, caraway seeds, mustard, and horseradish and mix on low until the mixture comes together. (No more than 2 minutes.)

3. Whisk Deli Rye Flavor and 4 cups flour together in a small bowl. Begin adding flour mixture 1 cup at a time, gently mixing on low to incorporate, about 2 minutes. Once you've added 3 cups of flour, increase the speed to medium-low and let the machine run for a minute. Stop the machine and touch the dough. If it is very sticky and wet, add ¼ cup of flour at a time until the dough is tacky but not wet to the touch.

4. Once dough reaches desired consistency, mix on medium until it is smooth and shiny, about 3 to 5 minutes.

5. Lightly brush a large mixing bowl with 1 tablespoon olive oil. Add the dough to the bowl and turn to coat. Cover with a clean towel or plastic wrap and let it rise in a warm spot until doubled in size, about 1 to 2 hours.

6. Preheat the oven to 375°F.

7 Grease a standard loaf pan with the remaining olive oil and place the dough inside. Allow the dough to proof and rise a second time until it has almost doubled in size, about 45 minutes to 1 hour.

8 Brush the dough with the beaten egg and bake in the oven, rotating the pan halfway through, until bread is golden brown and the inside of the loaf has reached 200°F on an instant read thermometer, about 1 hour.

9 Let cool completely before slicing into ¾-inch slices. (Or go for 1-inch slices if you're feeling greedy.) If you want the full-griddled experience, spread some softened butter (or beef, pork, or duck fat, you wild animal) on both sides of each slice. Heat up a large cast iron skillet or griddle over medium heat and toast those beautiful slices on each side until they are nice and golden, about 3 minutes a side. Then, add your patty and delicious toppings and be happy.

STORAGE NOTES: *Tightly wrapped bread will keep at room temperature for two to three days. This loaf also freezes well.*

TASTY WITH:

NYC Pastrami, Polish Beet Mustard, Pop's Russian, Spicy Garlic Pickles

BALLAH'

YIELD: 8 to 12 buns   START TO FINISH: 2 to 3 hours   ACTIVE TIME: 30 to 45 minutes

We realize there's an entire population of burger eaters out there who think brioche is the best bun for a burger. We aren't fooled, though. Brioche is generally way too much bread for a burger, so what should be a cloud-like masterpiece usually turns into a dense disaster under the weight of the patty. Sadly, the same goes for challah. While it's delicious on its own, it doesn't make much sense in burgerland.

But there is a reason why people are drawn to these breads; we can't ignore the fact that there is something about these flavors that works well with a burger. So we combined the best of both into one amazing bun. The airiness of a good brioche mixed with the eggy, sweet flavors of a traditional challah. It's *ballah'*, baby. A hybrid that can't be beat.

2½ teaspoons active dry yeast

2 teaspoons granulated sugar

⅓ cup warm milk (any will do, 100-110°F)

¼ cup honey

5 eggs (1 egg beaten with a fork in a small bowl, reserved)

3 teaspoons kosher salt

¼ cup olive oil, plus 1 tablespoon olive oil for greasing

6 tablespoons unsalted butter, cubed and softened

3½ to 5 cups all-purpose flour

1 Combine yeast, sugar, and ⅓ cup warm milk in a small bowl. Stir gently and allow the yeast to activate, about 5 minutes. You'll know it's ready when the yeast is foamy.

2 In a stand mixer with the dough hook attachment, add the yeast mixture, honey, 4 eggs, salt, ¼ cup olive oil, and butter and mix on low for no more than 2 minutes.

3 Add flour 1 cup at a time, gently mixing on low to incorporate. Once you've added 3 cups of flour, increase the speed to medium-low and let the machine run for a minute.

4 Stop the machine and touch the dough. If it is very sticky and wet, add more flour, ¼ cup at a time, and continue mixing for another minute. Continue in this fashion. Once the dough no longer feels wet, mix on medium until it is smooth and shiny, about 3 to 5 minutes.

5 Lightly brush a large mixing bowl with olive oil. Add the dough to the bowl and turn to coat. Cover with a clean towel or plastic wrap and let rise in a warm spot until doubled in size, about 1 hour.

6 Preheat the oven to 375°F.

7 Once dough has doubled in size, turn out onto a large, lightly floured surface, and divide into 12 pieces for smaller burgers or 8 pieces for larger burgers. Cover with a clean towel.

8 Working with 1 piece at a time (and keeping the remaining pieces covered until ready to use), shape the dough into discs. Place the discs onto a large baking sheet lined with parchment paper and repeat with the remaining dough. Don't crowd the buns on the baking sheet; use multiple baking sheets if necessary.

9 Allow the shaped buns to proof and rise for a second time, covered with a towel in a warm spot (right by the preheated oven would do the trick), until doubled in size, 15 to 20 minutes.

10 Brush each piece of dough with the beaten egg. Bake in the oven for about 10 to 12 minutes if making smaller buns (14 to 16 minutes if making larger buns), rotating the pan halfway through, until buns are golden brown and the interior temperature has reached 200°F on an instant read thermometer.

11 Cool slightly before cutting in half and topping with a burger. These are great fresh out of the oven but can also be warmed in a toaster oven with a little butter.

STORAGE NOTES: *Tightly wrapped buns will keep at room temperature for one to two days. They also freeze well.*

TASTY WITH:

Watercress, Chive & Cream Cheese Spread, Porterhouse Tartare, GGS Shiitakes

GLAZED DONUTS WITH FOIE-STING

YIELD: A baker's dozen   START TO FINISH: 2¼ hours   ACTIVE TIME: 45 minutes

Ahhh, the American glazed donut: a tender, sticky, melt-in-your-mouth symphony of sweet and yeasty harmony. Now imagine that delicious creation with a savory frosting of foie gras oozing down its sides. Ladies and gents, we present to you the most decadent burger bun imaginable. And the good news is that this recipe makes plenty, so you can enjoy some piping hot, gooey donuts straight out of the fryer with your burger or with your morning coffee the next day. Yum.

2½ teaspoons active dry yeast

¼ cup warm water (100-110°F)

2 eggs

⅓ cup vegetable shortening

½ cup granulated sugar

1½ cups whole milk

5 cups all-purpose flour

1 tablespoon olive oil

Pinch kosher salt

4 cups canola or peanut oil, for frying

FOIE-STING

⅓ pound foie gras, cut into 1-inch pieces

2 cups powdered sugar

3 tablespoons cold water

Pinch kosher salt

1 In a stand mixer with the dough hook attachment, combine yeast and ¼ cup warm water in a small bowl. Stir gently and allow the yeast to activate, about 5 minutes. You'll know it's ready when the yeast is foamy.

2 Add eggs, shortening, sugar, and milk to bowl. Using dough hook, mix on medium until eggs are beaten.

3 Set the mixer to lowest speed and add flour.

4 Once all ingredients are fully incorporated and resemble dough, knead in stand mixer for 2 more minutes. No more, no less. If your dough is overworked, the donuts will *not* melt in your mouth. Dough should be tacky but not stick to your fingers.

5 Lightly brush a large mixing bowl with olive oil, add the dough to the bowl, and turn to coat. Cover in plastic wrap and let rise for 1 hour.

6 On a floured surface, punch down dough into a ½-inch thick circular shape. Use a 3½-inch round ring mold or dough cutter to cut out donuts. Take care to cut donuts close together to minimize wasted edges. If you nail the ring placement, you'll yield 13 donuts. Please do not use the scraps. They are fucked.

7 Gently place donuts on a floured baking tray and let them rise again (uncovered) for 30 minutes.

8 Meanwhile, prepare glaze. (If your or your state's views toward animal rights restrict you from using foie gras, go ahead and make a traditional glaze. Simply substitute 6 tablespoons butter for foie gras and follow the steps as outlined here.) Place foie gras in a metal bowl over a pot

of boiling water and render until the fat has drained out, about 20 minutes. Strain the fat and discard the solids. In a clean bowl, add rendered foie gras (or butter) and remaining ingredients together and whisk until smooth.

9 Time to make the donuts! Heat the frying oil to 350°F (see Frying Guide on page xiv). Fry for exactly 3 minutes on each side. When it's time to flip, do so carefully with a metal spoon. Using a slotted spoon, transfer donuts to wire rack.

10 Grab your glaze of choice and pour over donuts while they are still warm, so the glaze is encouraged to melt a little and conform to every little spot on your donut's surface.

11 Allow glaze to set, approximately 2 minutes, then cut donut in half horizontally and use as a burger bun. Homer Simpson would be so proud.

STORAGE NOTES: *Store in an airtight container at room temperature for one day. Better yet: be a hero. Bring leftovers into work.*

TASTY WITH:

Fried Ketchup, 11-Hour Corned Beef Hash, Smoked Tasso Ham, Jammy Yolk

....

Add a slice of baby Swiss and a drizzle of maple syrup... Oh, yes! SEE NEXT PAGE →

MONTE CRISTO

FRIED KETCHUP →

Page 124

SMOKED
TASSO HAM →

Page 214

11-HOUR
CORNED BEEF HASH

Page 204

GLAZED DONUT
WITH FOIE-STING
Page 62

JAMMY YOLKS

Page 209

DRIZZLE OF
MAPLE SYRUP

**SLICE OF
BABY
SWISS**

4.
GOING ALL THE WHEY

VERMONT "VELVEETA" / PIMENTO EZ CHZ / SEMOLINA &
PANKO CRUSTED BURRATA / KING FRICO / KFC BUFFALO BLUE
CHEESE / BUTTERY BAKED ROBIOLA / $30 FONDUE /
WHITE TRASH CHEVRE / GOOEY JUCY LUCY / HUSHPUPPY
BATTERED CHILE RELLENOS

SOME SAY CHEESE is just a condiment—merely an option—but we say it's essential to the perfect burger. There is no gray area on this topic; there must be cheese and lots of it. It has to be melted, gooey, and indulgent.

While American cheese very clearly reigns supreme for its awesome meltability and uncanny willingness to become a divine sauce on top of your patty, there is a whole world of blue, funky, creamy, and sharp cheeses out there. What's more, there are ways to make those cheeses even better. (Impossible, you say. Just wait and see, say us.) So let's go all the whey. (If you aren't used to our piss-poor food puns by now, well, we don't know what to tell you.)

VERMONT "VELVEETA"

YIELD: 2½ cups   START TO FINISH: 12½ hours   ACTIVE TIME: 30 minutes

Dale Earnhardt is to NASCAR as Velveeta is to cheese. Legen-*dairy*. We're talking about pure, American glory here, folks. Frankly, we are offended by all of those loudmouth gourmets who have nothing but hate for processed cheese, claiming it's not "real." Well, we're here to call them out! Processed cheese is exactly that: cheese that is processed.

Maybe, just maybe, if we all join forces and start crafting our own homemade, processed cheeses using whole ingredients and artisan cheddars we can redeem the image of this beloved American delight. Be sure to have fun with this recipe, and if you're not too drunk, get the kids involved. It's great for them to see how food is made before getting packed into their convenient little Lunchables.

A few notes about this recipe's ingredients:

(1) It's imperative that you grate your own cheese. Convenient as it may seem, pre-shredded cheese just doesn't have the same zip and may affect the texture of the finished product. (2) Platinum gelatin is what we use in our professional kitchens, but it is readily accessible to home cooks. Save yourself the run-around and order it online. (3) And finally, liquid annatto—made from the seeds of achiote—will give this cheese that classic orange look. If you don't have a good spice or cheese-making supply shop nearby, it is readily available online. Or skip it and make white "Velveeta" instead of orange.

1 pound of your favorite Vermont cheddar, freshly grated by hand	① Put grated cheese in food processor.
	② Line an 8½-inch by 4½-inch loaf pan with plastic wrap and set aside.
4 sheets gelatin (platinum)	
1 cup whole milk	③ Bloom gelatin. Soak gelatin sheets in cold water for 7 minutes. After 7 minutes, gently squeeze out excess water.
⅛ teaspoon cream of tartar	
1 teaspoon kosher salt	④ In a 4-quart pot bring milk, gelatin, cream of tartar, and salt to a gentle simmer and whisk continuously for 30 seconds.
10 drops liquid annatto	
	⑤ Moving quickly so that liquid stays hot, turn food processor on and stream in milk mixture.
	⑥ Continue to process until cheese mixture becomes creamy and smooth, about 2 minutes.

7 Using a rubber spatula, pour cheese mixture into the lined loaf pan. Fold plastic wrap across top to seal edges.

8 Refrigerate until fully cooled and firm enough to slice, about 12 hours. Turn out onto a cutting board and cut into ½-inch thick slices, or thicker if you're a baller. Only cut as many slices as you need at the time. The rest of the loaf can be kept wrapped in the original loaf pan until ready to use.

9 After the last flip of the patty, top each with a slice of cheese. (But sneak an extra for yourself—that's what we like to call the "chef's cut.") Then wait for it to melt like orange gold.

STORAGE NOTES: *Wrapped cheese (sliced or whole as a loaf) will keep in the refrigerator for up to two weeks.*

TASTY WITH:

Astrid's Paleo Waffles, Red Rooster, Peameal Bacon, and a French omelette

....

Speaking of breakfast... SEE NEXT PAGE →

THE *Morning* AFTER

VERMONT "VELVEETA"

Page 68

PIMENTO EZ CHZ

YIELD: 2½ cups   START TO FINISH: 12½ hours   ACTIVE TIME: 30 minutes

Easy cheese. The beloved pasteurized cheese snack in a can that we've stockpiled in our basement safe rooms in preparation for the highly anticipated zombie apocalypse. Our only beef is the limited selection; and although we currently can't get enough of the Cheddar 'n Bacon flavor, eternity is a long time. Solitude can cause a man to become delusional, and eventually, turn his back on trusted friends. Bacon included.

So we decided to take a whack at developing our own line of flavors—pimento being one—for the sake of variety, sanity, and mankind in general. We've also hacked the canning process, which, as of right now, is classified information, and until the United States government grants us permission to share the secret of spray cheese, you'll just have to *spread* this on your next righteous burger.

1½ sheets gelatin (platinum)

½ loaf Vermont "Velveeta" cut into 1-inch cubes (page 68)

1 red bell pepper, roasted, peeled, seeded, and puréed

⅔ cup whole milk

½ teaspoon salt

⅛ teaspoon cream of tartar

10 drops liquid annatto

1. Bloom gelatin. Soak gelatin sheets in cold water for 7 minutes. After 7 minutes, gently squeeze out excess water and place gelatin sheets in a medium metal bowl. (It is important that the bowl is metal because you are going to create a double boiler).

2. Place all remaining ingredients into the metal bowl with gelatin.

3. Find a pot that the bowl fits over nicely (not too big, not too small), fill it ⅓ of the way with water, and bring water to a boil.

4. Once water is boiling, place metal bowl over pot (this is a double boiler) and whisk constantly until cheese is fully melted and mixture is smooth.

5. Pour mixture into serving jars (4-ounce mason jars work well) and refrigerate for 12 hours, or until gelatin sets and cheese is firm, bouncy, and spreadable.

STORAGE NOTES: *This cheese will keep in the refrigerator for up to one week.*

TASTY WITH:

Beef & Rosemary Biscuit, Kool-Aid Pickles, and
Old Fashioned Sarsaparilla on the side

SEMOLINA & PANKO CRUSTED BURRATA

YIELD: 4 fried cheese patties   START TO FINISH: 3½ to 4 hours   ACTIVE TIME: 30 minutes

Fried cheese? Yes, please! If four is not enough, simply double (or triple!) this recipe and fry in batches.

2 eggs

1 cup all-purpose flour

1 cup panko breadcrumbs

1 cup semolina flour

2 8-ounce balls fresh burrata
(fresh mozzarella works
as well)

4 cups canola or vegetable
oil, for frying

Kosher salt, to taste

1 Whisk the eggs and set aside.

2 Set up your assembly line: Line up 4 bowls and fill the first with flour, the second with the whisked eggs, the third with panko bread-crumbs, and the fourth with semolina. Place a cooling rack on top of a 9-inch by 13-inch sheet tray.

3 Carefully cut each ball of burrata in half and evenly coat with the contents of each bowl, starting with the flour and working your way through the whisked eggs, the panko breadcrumbs, and the semolina flour.

4 Place each half on a rack when done and repeat until you have breaded all the pieces of cheese.

5 Place the cheese in the freezer until fully frozen, at least 3 hours.

6 Heat the frying oil to 350°F (see Frying Guide on page xiv). Make sure you have your favorite comics on hand. (Preferably *Mother Goose and Grimm*. Unless you are a square; then proceed with the NASDAQ quotes.) Fry the 4 pieces of cheese on each side until golden brown, about 3 minutes per side.

7 Ensure cheese is not still frozen in the middle by checking the temperature with a quick read thermometer before removing from oil. Anything above 150°F and you're good to go.

8 Place cheese on the funnies and immediately season with salt.

9 Keep warm in a 200°F oven for up to 30 minutes, and top off the burger of your choice.

STORAGE NOTES: *Fried burrata is best enjoyed right away. The frozen and breaded balls of burrata (through step 4) can be kept frozen for up to two months. Proceed with the recipe starting with step 5.*

TASTY WITH:

Pizza Stromboli Bun, Raw Kale Sofrito,
Charred Cherry Pepper Relish

KING FRICO

YIELD: 6 fricos   START TO FINISH: 40 minutes

It's hard to beat a proper Parmigiano-Reggiano, a versatile masterpiece and the undisputed king of Italian cheeses. When grated and baked, it turns into a magical cheese crisp that the Italians call a frico. Make a good, old fashioned hamburger and top with a frico or two for a crunchy bit of cheese heaven, or go the extra mile and top a cheese-drenched patty with a frico for a double hit of cheese pleasure.

1½ cups Parmigiano-Reggiano
   (about 6 ounces), freshly
   grated by hand

1 Preheat the oven to 375°F.

2 Line a baking sheet with a 16-inch by 11-inch silicone baking mat or parchment paper.

3 Make 6 piles of cheese on the baking mat, measuring 3 inches in diameter. (We use a ¼-cup measuring cup for portioning.) Leave an additional 1½-inch radius around each pile to accommodate them when they melt.

4 Bake until deep golden brown, about 6 to 10 minutes.

5 Allow fricos to cool for 20 minutes before handling.

6 Using an offset spatula or spoon, remove the cooled discs and place on burger.

STORAGE NOTES: *Fricos will keep for up to one week in an airtight container.*

TASTY WITH:

Grilled Romaine Hearts, Smoked Heirlooms,
Pepperoncini Cubanelles

KFC BUFFALO BLUE CHEESE

YIELD: About 4 cups of cheese and fried chicken regret   START TO FINISH: 45 minutes

We've all been there. That dark place called fast food shame. If you're like us, you treat yourself to a life-ending, grimy supper about twice a year, usually on a Friday night after drinking the town dry. You might be the only asshole walking through the drive-through, but that is the least of your worries. Once you step foot inside your favorite processed food fantasy, you panic, black out, and order the entire menu.

 The next day you awaken—ridden with guilt, forty-six dollars lighter, and swimming in soggy, deep-fried leftovers. Here, we offer you a way to repurpose the contents of all those cartons without skipping your Saturday afternoon cookout with the guys.

6 pieces KFC Extra Crispy Tenders, preferably purchased in shame (or 6 pieces store-bought frozen chicken tenders, prepared according to package)

4 KFC Creamy Buffalo Dip'ems (or ½ cup Frank's Red Hot Sauce)

8 ounces blue cheese

8 ounces cream cheese, room temperature

½ teaspoon kosher salt

1 teaspoon celery seed

2 teaspoons freshly cracked black pepper

1. Preheat oven to 400°F.

2. Cut the chicken strips into a medium dice and eat a few little num nums as a treat. You deserve it.

3. Place half of the diced chicken in a medium mixing bowl and the other half in a food processor.

4. Add Buffalo Dip'ems (or hot sauce), blue cheese, cream cheese, salt, celery seed, and pepper to the chicken in the food processor. Pureé until smooth.

5. Scrape the pureéd mixture into the bowl with the chopped chicken and mix well.

6. Pour mixture into a 6-inch cast iron skillet on top of a baking sheet (don't you dare share any of that cheese with your oven floor), and bake for 30 minutes. Boom shakalaka!

7. Do what you know you want to do and slather this creation all over a burger while this cheesy delight is still warm. (Or go way lowbrow and use as a dip.)

STORAGE NOTES: *Cooked and cooled dip can remain in the cast iron skillet or an airtight container in the refrigerator for up to one week. Reheat at 400°F until warm, about ten to fifteen minutes. You can also gently reheat the cheese in a medium saucepan over medium-low heat until warmed through, about ten to fifteen minutes.*

TASTY WITH:

Lowcountry Cornbread, Crispy Leeks, and your hangover

BUTTERY BAKED ROBIOLA

YIELD: 4 pieces baked Robiola START TO FINISH: 45 minutes

Baked Robiola is absolutely delightful on top of a burger. You will have instantly upped your cheese game and your burger will thank you for it. This is an easy recipe to double so don't hold back.

12 sheets phyllo dough, thawed

4 tablespoons unsalted butter, melted

Kosher salt, to taste

8 ounces Robiola, cut into 4 equal squares (if you can't find Robiola, use a good quality brie)

1. Preheat oven to 350°F.

2. Cut phyllo dough into a 6-inch square and save extra trimmings for another use.

3. On a clean workspace, lay down 1 sheet and gently brush with butter. Place second sheet on top of first sheet and brush with butter. Repeat until you've buttered and layered 3 sheets, then season top sheet with salt.

4. Place one Robiola square in the center of the phyllo, flatten cheese to match the size of your patty, and fold corners of phyllo inward until they meet, creating a sealed pouch. Brush any dry bits of phyllo with butter. Place on a parchment-lined baking sheet.

5. Repeat until all 4 cheese squares are wrapped in phyllo.

6. Bake until deeply golden brown all over, about 20-25 minutes.

7. Best served warm and crispy, straight from the oven. However, you can keep warm in a 200°F oven for up to 30 minutes before topping your burger. Once cooled, they can be reheated in a 325°F oven until hot, about 8 to 12 minutes.

STORAGE NOTES: *Baked Robiola will keep in the refrigerator for up to one week. The unbaked squares can be prepared in advance and kept in the refrigerator for up to one week, or in the freezer for up to one month. Add an extra eight to twelve minutes to the cooking time if they go straight from the freezer to the oven.*

TASTY WITH:

Portlandia Dry Rub,
Ballah',
Red Onion
Marmalade

$30 FONDUE

YIELD: 4 cups   START TO FINISH: 20 to 30 minutes

Last time we checked, two artisan-made cheeses and a four-pack of craft beer ran us about $38. It may seem egregious for fondue, but still. You should try it. Live the good life every now and again.

Feel free to cut the recipe in half and enjoy the other half wheel of Harbison in a more civilized manner. Or pretend to be Betty Draper for a night and just serve this dish as straight fondue. However, if you want to live out all your dark burger fantasies, ladle on the cheese like you're made of money.

4 tablespoons unsalted butter

6 tablespoons all-purpose flour

2 cups pilsner (we like Dogfish Head Piercing Pils)

1 pound Taleggio, rind removed, diced into 1-inch pieces

10 ounces Jasper Hill Harbison, rind on, diced into 1-inch pieces (if you need to substitute, look for a soft, funky cheese)

1 teaspoon kosher salt

3 teaspoons freshly cracked black pepper

Pinch ground nutmeg

Smidgen ground allspice

1 In a saucepot over medium heat, melt butter then whisk in flour.

2 When the butter and flour mixture turns golden brown, pour in the cold beer and add the cheeses.

3 Whisk everything together until the cheese is melted and the mixture is creamy, about 5 to 8 minutes.

4 Add remaining seasonings just before serving. Smother it on, under, and all over that filthy burger. Once slightly cooled, pour the contents into an airtight container. Gently reheat as needed over low heat in a medium pot until warmed through, 8 to 12 minutes.

STORAGE NOTES: *Cheese will keep in an airtight container for up to one week.*

TASTY WITH:

Bacon, Scallion & Cream Cheese English Muffin, Vidalia Jam, Pan Fried Pickled Green Tomatoes

WHITE TRASH CHEVRE

Yield: 6 patties   Start to finish: 10 to 15 minutes

You could use this spread to make some tasty hors d'oeuvres with pickles and toothpicks at your next redneck party, but the better bet is to schmear it all over every nook and cranny of your patty and give that slab of ground cattle the proper send off to white trash heaven it deserves.

A couple of notes: You probably don't want to add anything else except fresh, raw vegetables to the completed burger. This stuff is rich and super cheesy—and it might be the reason why you don't show up for work in the morning. This recipe calls for your favorite pork rinds, so grab a big bag of any brand you like and snack away as you cook.

8 ounces chevre-style goat cheese, softened at room temperature

12 Kosher Dill Chips, roughly chopped (page 171)

¼ cup KC Pit Master (page 139)

½ cup chicharrones, crushed

1. Get drunk off something cheap and in a can.

2. Mix goat cheese with pickles and BBQ sauce.

3. Divide into 6 equal balls and form into patties. Coat both sides of the patties with the crushed chicharrones.

4. Place the chevre patties on your burgers. Don't forget to call your boss before you pass out.

Storage Notes: *Eat them right away or they will get nasty.*

TASTY WITH:
Mashed Potato & Gravy Roll and all the fresh veg you can get your hands on

GOOEY JUCY LUCY

YIELD: 4 huge burgers   START TO FINISH: 30 minutes

Our one exception to the "stuffed" burger rule is the Jucy Lucy—created and deliberately misspelled by the good folks at Matt's Bar in Minneapolis.

When you stuff cheese between two beef patties, the result is a gushing and stretchy cheesy center that is burger bliss. Finishing the burger in the oven will properly melt the cheese, but keep in mind—your burger must cook to well done in order to ensure a melty center.

The inside is like an active volcano, so do yourself a favor and let it rest before taking a bite. Otherwise you run the risk of spilling ridiculously hot beef juices all over your face, or worse, getting a scorching cheese mustache that will Freddy Krueger your upper lip for weeks.

36 ounces ground beef

Kosher salt and freshly ground black pepper, to taste

½ pound Gruyere, rind removed, sliced into 4 4-inch squares, 1 inch thick

A splash canola or vegetable oil

1 Preheat the oven to 375°F.

2 Form your beef into 8 4½-ounce flat patties that are 4 inches in diameter. Season them on both sides with salt and pepper.

3 Using a 3-inch diameter cookie cutter, cut out 4 circles of cheese that will fit inside the patty, leaving about a ½-inch border of meat.

4 Place a cheese circle on top of each patty, making sure each slice fits inside the beef with enough room to have a border of just beef.

5 Top with the remaining patties, sandwiching the cheese. Crimp the edges of the patties to create a complete seal. Make sure it is tight and no cheese is visible, otherwise the burger will burst during cooking and you'll lose all that cheese in the cooking process.

6 Get your cast iron skillet ripping hot over medium-high heat for a couple of minutes.

7 Add the burger and cook, without flipping, until the cooked side is golden brown and lovely, about 4 to 6 minutes. Carefully flip the burger and transfer the pan to the oven and finish cooking for 7 minutes.

8 The Jucy Lucys are done when the center has reached a temperature of 160°F. Use your instant read thermometer.

9 Let the burgers rest for about 5 minutes while you prepare your buns and toppings. Assemble, take a bite, and enjoy the onslaught of cheese headed your way.

TASTY WITH:

Ballah', Bacon & Beer Honey Mustard, Full Sours

HUSHPUPPY BATTERED CHILE RELLENOS

YIELD: 4 rellenos   START TO FINISH: 3½ to 4 hours   ACTIVE TIME: About 45 minutes

Pirates loved hushpuppies; Blackbeard was no exception. He used to hide out off the coast of the Outer Banks in North Carolina on Ocracoke Island, munching these delicious treats. We modeled this batter after North Carolina style hushpuppies. They're far moister than that swashbuckler Blackbeard's were. Next time you're in North Carolina, leave a plate behind as tribute. (With a bottle of rum.)

These hushpuppies are slightly sweet, slightly spicy, and should only be made with Texas Pete hot sauce, which (contrary to what its name suggests) is made in North Carolina. Ok, fine. If you wanna be fussy and use a different hot sauce, just make sure you're using a Louisiana-style red hot—or else.

If needed, double this recipe and fry in batches (four for you and four for everyone else to share).

4 poblano chile peppers

4 ounces cotija cheese, cut into 1-inch strips

4 ounces chihuahua or jack cheese, shredded

1 cup all-purpose flour

¾ cup corn flour

½ teaspoon baking powder

¼ cup granulated sugar

1 cup buttermilk

4 eggs

1½ teaspoons freshly cracked black pepper

1 teaspoon kosher salt, plus more to taste

20 dashes Texas Pete hot sauce

4 cups canola or vegetable oil, for frying

1. Roast chiles by placing them over the flame of a grill or gas stove-top burner for about 20 minutes total, turning the chiles every couple of minutes to make sure they are evenly charred. (Alternatively, you can roast them in the oven at 450°F until charred all over, about 20 to 30 minutes.) Cut off the tops, remove the seeds, and set chiles aside until they are cool enough to handle.

2. Stuff the roasted chiles with cotija and chihuahua cheeses and place in freezer until fully frozen, at least 3 hours.

3. In the meantime, make hushpuppy batter by combining flours, baking powder, sugar, buttermilk, eggs, pepper, 1 teaspoon salt, and hot sauce in a medium bowl. Whisk together until smooth and refrigerate until ready to use.

4. Once rellenos are frozen, heat the frying oil to 350°F (see Frying Guide on page xiv). Keep a brown paper bag and salt close by.

5. Take batter out of the refrigerator and whisk for 10 to 15 seconds to allow it to loosen and regain that smooth texture.

6. Using 2 forks, dip each relleno into the hushpuppy batter and coat all over. Quickly and carefully move the batter-dipped rellenos to the fryer.

7 Fry until batter is deep golden brown on the outside and cheese is melty on the inside, about 8 to 10 minutes. (Ensure cheese is not still frozen in middle by checking the temperature with an instant read thermometer before removing from oil. Anything above 150°F and you're good to go.)

8 Place rellenos on brown paper bag and immediately season with salt. Repeat frying and seasoning until you've cooked all 4 rellenos.

9 Keep the rellenos warm in a 200°F oven for up to 30 minutes until ready to use, and then top off your favorite burger.

STORAGE NOTES: *The hushpuppies are best enjoyed right away. The stuffed chiles (through step 2) can be frozen for up to two months. When you are ready to fry them, proceed with step 3. The batter will last for about a day in the refrigerator.*

YOU'LL HAVE ENOUGH hushpuppy batter left over to whip up a nice side dish or appetizer! Pour leftover hushpuppy batter into the fryer through a funnel (any size will do). Make the hushpuppies as small or as large as you'd like. Fry in batches until golden brown and firm, about 3 to 4 minutes per batch. Place on paper bag, season with salt, and enjoy! These go fantastically with Mark's Ill Dip, page 149.

TASTY WITH: Southwest Mole Negro, Texas Frito Pie Crumble, IPA Sesame Seed Bun, Salsa Quemada, Mark's Ill Dip—*add some shred-ded iceberg lettuce and nacho chips if you're really badass.* SEE NEXT PAGE →

THE

NACHO LIBRE

STARRING

SALSA QUEMADA

Page 101

SOUTHWEST MOLE NEGRO

Page 23

TEXAS **FRITO PIE** CRUMBLE

Page 31

HUSHPUPPY BATTERED

 # CHILE RELLENO

Page 86

SHREDDED ICEBERG LETTUCE ✦ MARK'S ILL DIP

Page 149

ON AN

IPA SESAME SEED BUN

Page 38

5.

LTO INTERMEZZO

RAW KALE SOFRITO / WATERCRESS, CHIVE & CREAM CHEESE
SPREAD / GRILLED ROMAINE HEARTS / POP'S DIRTY SLAW /
SALSA QUEMADA / SMOKED HEIRLOOMS / CHERRY TOMATO
HOT SAUCE / PAN FRIED PICKLED GREEN TOMATOES /
CHARRED MARINATED SCALLIONS / QUICK PICKLED RED
ONIONS / VIDALIA JAM / CRISPY LEEKS

OFTEN SERVED AS a palate cleanser during a multicourse dinner, an intermezzo should be bright and stimulating. The addition of fresh lettuce, tomato, and onion to a rich, fatty burger might seem like the obvious connection to our wordplay, but this intermezzo is meant to be refreshing in a more philosophical sense.

We appreciate and love the addition of seasonal, mouthwatering vegetables, and we can get behind running our burgers "through the garden," but only to a certain point. For the life of us, we are not quite sure why iceberg lettuce, out-of-season tomatoes, and the ubiquitous raw onion became the standard garnish for burgers nationwide when there is a whole world of creativity out there.

Don't fret if your summer veggie season is shorter than Larry Bird's shorts or heirlooms are hard to come by; there are plenty of easy ways to bring a crisp vegetal addition to your burgers any time of year. The recipes in this chapter elevate your run-of-the-mill LTO, giving you a topping that has earned a right to grace that amazing patty. Ditch those sad greens—it's time to get your vegetation on.

LETTUCE

Let's face the music. Iceberg lettuce is like staying in on a Friday night. It feels right from time to time, but once it becomes a habit, you grow old and die. Here we give you some easy ways to utilize the vibrant greens available to you, no matter what month it is.

....

RAW KALE SOFRITO

YIELD: About 1 cup   START TO FINISH: 10 minutes

8 kale leaves (stems removed), roughly chopped

¼ cup fresh parsley, roughly chopped

¼ cup fresh cilantro, roughly chopped

2 tablespoons fresh dill, roughly chopped

2 tablespoons fresh mint, roughly chopped

2 tablespoons freshly squeezed lemon juice

Zest of 1 lemon

¼ cup extra virgin olive oil

Kosher salt and freshly cracked black pepper, to taste

1 Place all ingredients in food processor and pulse until finely chopped but still somewhat coarse. (It's a lot easier to get the desired consistency when placing everything in the processor already roughly chopped.)

2 Season to taste with salt and pepper and spread it over your burger bun.

STORAGE NOTES: *Sofrito will retain its bright green color when stored in an airtight container in the refrigerator for up to two days.*

TASTY WITH:

Ballah', Buttery Baked Robiola, Smoked Tasso Ham

WATERCRESS, CHIVE & CREAM CHEESE SPREAD

YIELD: About 1 cup START TO FINISH: 5 to 10 minutes

1 bunch watercress,
   roughly chopped

1 bunch chives,
   roughly chopped

8 ounces cream cheese at
   room temperature

½ lemon, juice and zest

Kosher salt and freshly
   cracked black pepper,
   to taste

1. Place all ingredients in food processor and purée until smooth. (It's a lot easier to get the desired consistency when placing everything in the processor already roughly chopped.)

2. Season to taste with salt and pepper and spread it on your burger bun.

STORAGE NOTES: *Spread will keep in the refrigerator for up to three days.*

TASTY WITH:

Bacon, Scallion & Cream Cheese English Muffin,
Jammy Yolks, Peameal Bacon

GRILLED ROMAINE HEARTS

YIELD: About 2 cups   START TO FINISH: 15 minutes

1 heart romaine lettuce

Kosher salt and freshly cracked
   black pepper, to taste

2 tablespoons light olive oil
   or canola oil

1. Preheat grill to highest temperature setting; or, if you have a gas stovetop range, lay a roasting rack over your burner and turn on high.

2. Split romaine heart in half, but keep the core and root end intact. This will help hold it together while grilling.

3. Season the flat, cut side with salt and pepper and brush with oil.

4. Place seasoned, oiled side down onto grill and cook until grill marks are achieved, about 2 to 3 minutes. Remove lettuce before it becomes wilted.

5. Remove the root end and slice into ½-inch strips.

STORAGE NOTES: *Grilled romaine should be eaten right away.*

TASTY WITH:

White Bread, Smoked Heirlooms, Vidalia Jam, Red Remoulade, Chicken Fried Pork Belly

....

How about a burger BLT...? SEE NEXT PAGE →

BLT Club

VIDALIA JAM
Page 111

SMOKED HEIRLOOMS
Page 102

WHITE AMERICAN CHEESE

WHITE BREAD

GRILLED
ROMAINE
HEARTS
Page 95

CHICKEN FRIED
PORK BELLY
Page 212

RED REMOULADE
Page 136

SAMMY HERE. When I was in high school, I was a line cook at Bud & Eb's, my parents' bar and grill in Chapel Hill. This slaw recipe is something my pops and I developed together, and every time I taste it, it brings back great memories.

We used to make shaved BBQ pork po' boys with cheddar, caramelized onions, Kansas City-style BBQ sauce, and this Louisiana slaw; they were the bomb! One Sunday, when my parents went out of town, I snuck into the restaurant with a clan of teenagers. With no supervision, we quickly descended on the beer taps as if they were trying to escape.

Things escalated. In the walk-in cooler, I discovered a small wolf pack of drunken high school seniors chowing down on ice-cold, half-cooked chicken wings. It was at this moment that I realized we needed food, so I fired up the kitchen and took orders. After conducting a quick survey, the decision was unanimous: BBQ pork sandos for all!

It's a shame that loyal patrons can no longer indulge in that slammin' sandwich. Anyone who ever had even one bite of that po' boy would agree—it was Pop's dirty version of Louisiana slaw that made it so memorable. Toss it on your burger, your sandwich, or on the side of a dog or grilled sausage. Make this slaw and make a memory.

POP'S DIRTY SLAW

YIELD: 6 to 8 cups   START TO FINISH: 20 minutes

½ head large cabbage, thinly sliced

½ red onion, thinly sliced

½ bunch scallions, thinly sliced

6 large leaves collard greens (tough stems removed), sliced into a chiffonade

½ jalapeño, minced (seeds in or out, up to you)

2 cloves garlic, minced

2 teaspoons granulated sugar

2 teaspoons kosher salt

2 teaspoons freshly cracked black pepper

¼ cup Bourbon Barrel Red Hot (page 142 or Tabasco)

¼ cup Foolproof Whole Grain Mustard (page 127 or store-bought)

1 cup Creole Mayo (page 135)

1 Combine all ingredients in a large bowl and mix thoroughly, incorporating everything.

2 Refrigerate for at least 3 hours before eating so that flavors can marry. (This slaw tastes best the next day and gets even better after 2 days.)

STORAGE NOTES: *Slaw will keep in the refrigerator for up to one week.*

TASTY WITH:

Mashed Potato & Gravy Roll, KFC Buffalo Blue Cheese

TOMATO

August tomatoes are a thing of beauty. Firm, juicy, and colorful, these sweet little fruits are perfect when sliced, seasoned, and tucked into a burger. While tomato elitists everywhere turn their backs on tomatoes from October to July, we embrace year-round tomato consumption—especially on a burger! We're not endorsing throwing a weird winter tomato naked onto your burger, but you can still step up your game with a less-than-pristine piece of fruit.

SALSA QUEMADA

YIELD: 2 cups   START TO FINISH: 1 hour

1 lime, zest and juice

3 tablespoons freshly cracked black pepper, divided

½ bunch cilantro, leaves and stems, roughly chopped

1 tablespoon light olive oil or canola oil, for lubrication

Kosher salt, to taste

1 pound ripe Roma tomatoes

1 red onion, cut into quarters

1 jalapeño

1 poblano chile pepper

1 bunch scallions

4 garlic cloves

1. Fire up your grill.

2. Place the lime juice and zest in a blender with 1 teaspoon black pepper and cilantro. Set aside. (Do not blend yet, you're just setting yourself up for upcoming steps.)

3. Lightly oil all vegetables and season to taste with salt and 2 teaspoons of black pepper.

4. Char all vegetables on grill until as much surface area as possible is black but not burnt. (Burnt means dried out, crunchy, bitter, and flavorless. That's going too far.)

5. Once all vegetables are charred, add to blender and purée until you reach your favorite salsa consistency.

6. Season to taste with salt. You can also add more black pepper if you like.

STORAGE NOTES: *Salsa will keep in the refrigerator for up to five days.*

TASTY WITH:

Gorditas, Hushpuppy Battered Chile Rellenos, Avocado Ranch

SMOKED HEIRLOOMS

YIELD: Tomato slices for 4 burgers   START TO FINISH: 5 minutes

Here's your chance to finally play with that smoking gun you asked Santa for. It's a great little tool for cold smoking things indoors. Adult supervision required, of course. This recipe also uses your favorite smoking chips—grab some leftovers from that ridiculously tasty hot sauce you just made (page 142).

2 heirloom tomatoes, sliced
⅓-inch thick

1½ teaspoons good quality
sea salt

SPECIAL EQUIPMENT:

Smoking gun
Smoking chips

1. Lay tomatoes on a sheet tray and cover tightly with plastic wrap.

2. Peel back one corner and place smoking tube inside. Wrap plastic around tube so no smoke can escape the chamber you have just created.

3. Stoke gun and generate smoke for 15 seconds. Quickly remove tube and lock in smoke by sealing tray with plastic. Allow tomatoes to cold smoke for 2 minutes. Repeat.

4. Season with sea salt and stack them high on your burger.

STORAGE NOTES: *Best eaten the same day you make them.*

TASTY WITH:

Ultimate Jewish Rye Bread, $30 Fondue,
Horseradish Half Sours

CHERRY TOMATO HOT SAUCE

YIELD: 1½ cups   START TO FINISH: 5 minutes

4 ounces cherry tomatoes
(about ½ carton)

1 Fresno chile

1 habanero

2 cloves garlic

½ cup freshly squeezed lime
juice (about 4 limes)

¼ cup water

1 teaspoon kosher salt

1. Purée all ingredients in blender for 2 minutes.

2. Pass through a fine mesh sieve.

STORAGE NOTES: *Sauce will keep in the refrigerator for up to two weeks.*

TASTY WITH:
Cali Asada, Gorditas, Pimento EZ CHZ

PAN FRIED PICKLED GREEN TOMATOES

YIELD: 8 slices of tomatoes   START TO FINISH: About 10 minutes

¼ cup light olive oil or
   canola oil

8 slices Pickled Green Tomatoes,
   ⅓-inch thick (page 191)

¼ cup corn flour

¼ cup all-purpose flour

2 teaspoons smoked paprika

Kosher salt and freshly cracked
   black pepper, to taste

1. Pour oil into a large cast iron skillet and place over medium-high heat.

2. Remove tomatoes from brine and pat dry with paper towel.

3. In a medium bowl, mix corn flour, flour, and paprika. Dredge each slice of tomato in the mixture.

4. Place tomato slices in the pan, leaving 1 inch between each slice. Fry in batches if necessary.

5. Fry until the tomatoes are golden brown on both sides, about 6 to 8 minutes total.

6. Place fried slices on paper towels and immediately season with salt and pepper.

STORAGE NOTES: *Best enjoyed right away.*

TASTY WITH:

IPA Sesame Seed Bun, "Cool Ranch" Ranch, Smoked Tasso Ham

ONION

When and why did raw onions become a key staple on American burgers? Onions are great—and we cook with them every day. (Key word: *cook*.) While they're tasty raw, their zesty bite can be more pungent than intended. Different members of the allium family have different levels of intensity, as well as their own unique flavor profiles. Don't be stuck with the same old, played-out, raw onion on every burger you craft. Unleash the true power of the onion!

CHARRED MARINATED SCALLIONS

YIELD: About ¾ cup   START TO FINISH: At least 1 hour   ACTIVE TIME: 10 minutes

2 bunches scallions

2 tablespoons light olive oil
    or canola oil

Kosher salt and freshly cracked
    black pepper, to taste

1 tablespoon ginger, minced

3 cloves garlic, thinly sliced

1 tablespoon rice wine vinegar

1 tablespoon soy sauce

½ teaspoon fish sauce

1 Preheat grill to highest temperature, or if you have a gas stovetop range, lay a roasting rack over your burner and turn on high.

2 Remove root ends of the scallions and discard. Lightly toss scallions with oil and season with salt and pepper.

3 Place scallions over heat and char evenly on both sides without completely burning them to an ashy crisp.

4 Remove, cool, and chop into 1-inch pieces.

5 Toss in a bowl with all remaining ingredients and marinate at room temperature for at least 1 hour.

6 Refrigerate until needed. Tastes best the next day.

STORAGE NOTES: *Scallions will keep in the refrigerator for up to five days.*

TASTY WITH:

Mashed Potato &
Gravy Roll,

Buttery Baked Robiola,

Red Rooster

QUICK PICKLED RED ONIONS

YIELD: About 2 cups   START TO FINISH: 3 hours   ACTIVE TIME: 5 minutes

1 red onion

1 lime, juice and zest

Kosher salt and freshly cracked
  black pepper, to taste

1 Using a mandolin or an extremely sharp knife, cut onion in half and shave paper-thin.

2 Toss onions in a bowl with lime juice and zest. Work ingredients together with your fingers until all the sliced onions are coated. Season to taste with salt and pepper.

3 Refrigerate until onions are a bright pinkish-purple and somewhat translucent, about 3 hours.

STORAGE NOTES: *Onions will keep in the refrigerator for at least two weeks.*

TASTY WITH:

Southwest Mole Negro, Gorditas, Creamy Chimichurri,
Coconut Sweet Potato Tots

VIDALIA JAM

YIELD: 2 cups   START TO FINISH: 1 hour

2 Vidalia onions, thinly sliced

1 tablespoon light olive oil
   or canola oil

¼ cup light brown sugar

¼ cup Worcestershire
   (page 145 or store-bought)

1 teaspoon kosher salt

2 teaspoons freshly cracked
   black pepper

1. In a medium pot, over medium-low heat, slowly caramelize onions with oil, about 25 minutes.

2. Once the onions have caramelized, add the rest of the ingredients. Simmer until Worcestershire has reduced into a syrupy liquid and the color of the onions is a deep brown, about 25 to 30 minutes.

3. Tastes best at room temperature or chilled.

STORAGE NOTES: *Jam will keep in the refrigerator for up to two weeks.*

TASTY WITH:

Dan's Memphis Rib Rub, Mashed Potato & Gravy Roll,
Crispy Leeks, Mark's Ill Dip

CRISPY LEEKS

Yield: 2½ cups   Start to finish: 20 minutes

Pile these tasty leeks on top of your burger to add a world of flavor and texture that is, frankly, hard to describe in words.

2 leeks

4 cups canola oil, for frying

Kosher salt, to taste

1 Remove the root ends from the leeks and discard. Cut the leeks into 3-inch sections, moving from whitish-green section up toward dark leafy stalks. (Do not use leafy stalks.) Then slice down the middle to create two long halves. Rinse in cold water to remove any grit or dirt.

2 Handling 2 to 3 layers at a time, julienne leeks as thin as possible. Place in cold water and repeat until all leeks are cut. Drain leeks and pat dry with paper towels.

3 Heat the oil to 350°F (see Frying Guide on page xiv). Fry leeks in small batches. With a slotted spoon, agitate leeks while in the fryer. Remove once they become a deep, dark brown.

4 Place leeks on brown paper bag and immediately season with salt. Repeat until all are fried. Top your beastly patty with a haystack of pleasure and chow down.

Storage Notes: *Best enjoyed right away.*

TASTY WITH:

IPA Sesame Seed Bun, Pop's Dirty Slaw, Mignonette Ketchup, Johnnycake Fried Oysters SEE NEXT PAGE →

MASON DIXON
MIXUP

CRISPY LEEKS

Page 113

JOHNNYCAKE
FRIED OYSTERS

Page 211

6.

ADDICTED TO THE SAUCE

KETCHUP / MUSTARD / MAYO / BBQ SAUCE / REFRIGERATOR
DOOR / SECRET STASH

THE CONDIMENT WAS placed on this earth for one reason and one reason alone: to serve the almighty burger. While a great burger is worthy of worship all by itself, there is a huge difference between what you need on a burger and what you want on a burger. We're sinners for the sauce. In fact, we're downright addicted.

Certain condiments complement certain burgers well, and flavor profiles are a personal, intimate affair. There is a staggering variety of spirited, easy-to-make condiments out there that will take you beyond ketchup, mustard, or mayonnaise, turning your fridge door into a treasure trove of saucy goodness that will dress your burger—and almost anything else you whip up in your kitchen.

KETCHUP

Good ole' Heinz ketchup was our first foray into the wonderful world of condiments—and we slurped it up as if it were its own food group. Once we got a taste of that tangy, sticky, sweet sauce, we couldn't get enough. Growing up, we dumped it on everything from chicken nuggets to fish sticks.

Because of the enduring popularity of Heinz, homemade ketchup is a tricky subject. Heinz is reliably consistent and nearly impossible to replicate. (And who would be brazen enough to try?) But in the world of ketchup, it's far from the only flavor out there. Basic ketchup is just the point of departure. So although we swear by Heinz, there is power in the homemade, and we're going to explore some of those delicious possibilities here.

UMAMI KETCHUP

YIELD: About 4 cups   START TO FINISH: About 3 hours   ACTIVE TIME: 25 to 30 minutes

4 Roma tomatoes

2 tablespoons olive oil, divided

Kosher salt and freshly cracked black pepper, to taste

1 small red onion, diced

4 anchovies packed in oil, minced into a paste

⅓ cup tomato paste

2 cloves black garlic, crushed (or substitute 2 cloves fresh garlic)

½ cup apple cider vinegar

½ cup brown sugar

⅓ cup Worcestershire (page 145 or store-bought)

14-ounce can crushed tomatoes

1. Preheat the oven to 375°F.

2. Slice the Roma tomatoes lengthwise into 3 or 4 slices and lay them on a parchment-lined baking sheet. Drizzle with 1 tablespoon olive oil and season with a pinch of salt and pepper.

3. Roast tomatoes in the oven for 30 minutes. Spoon any juices that have leaked out back onto the tomatoes.

4. Lower the heat to 325°F and continue roasting the tomatoes until they are completely soft and collapsed, about 45 minutes to 1 hour.

5. Meanwhile, heat the remaining olive oil in a saucepan over medium heat. Add the onion and cook until softened and translucent, about 3 to 5 minutes. Add the anchovies, tomato paste, and black garlic, stirring to coat. Cook until fragrant, about 1 minute.

6. Add the remaining ingredients, including a pinch of salt and pepper, and bring the mixture to a boil.

7. Reduce the heat to low and simmer for about 1 hour, adding the tomatoes when they are done roasting.

8. Cool slightly, then purée in a blender, adjusting the seasoning with salt, vinegar, and sugar as desired.

STORAGE NOTES: *Ketchup will keep in the refrigerator for up to one month.*

MIGNONETTE KETCHUP

YIELD: About 2 cups START TO FINISH: 20 minutes

You can't beat this: Start with the Umami Ketchup and add a traditional mignonette to up the acidity. Throw in whole oysters for brininess and depth, fish them out at the end, and slurp 'em down. As they glide past your lips, they will leave a trail of this amazing ketchup in their wake.

2 cups Umami Ketchup (page 119 or Heinz)

4 fresh oysters, scrubbed well, unshucked

¼ cup red wine vinegar

2 tablespoons shallot, minced (about 1 medium-sized shallot)

½ teaspoon freshly cracked black pepper

1 Bring the Umami Ketchup to a simmer and add the oysters.

2 Combine the remaining ingredients in a small bowl and add to the ketchup.

3 Simmer on low heat. Keep covered until the oysters begin to open, about 15 to 20 minutes.

4 Remove the oysters, keeping any residual oyster liquid in the pot. (But don't waste the little suckers! Here's that cook's treat we mentioned: shuck the oysters and slurp away!)

5 Taste for seasoning and enjoy with your favorite burger.

STORAGE NOTES: *This ketchup is best consumed within one to two days.*

BLOODY MARY KETCHUP

YIELD: About 4 cups   START TO FINISH: 1 hour

We love brunch as much as the next guy or gal, but who says we can't enjoy the flavors of a good Bloody Mary in the evening? Here, we take the zip and tang of that beloved morning cocktail and serve up a ketchup that packs a boozy punch any morning, noon, or night.

2 tablespoons olive oil

1 small red onion, diced

2 stalks celery, diced

Kosher salt and freshly cracked
   black pepper, to taste

2 cloves garlic, minced

1 teaspoon fresh ginger, peeled
   and roughly chopped

1 tablespoon celery seed

Pinch ground allspice

Pinch ground clove

6 ounces tomato paste

3 pickled jalapeños, chopped
   plus ¼ cup of their liquid

1 teaspoon prepared
   horseradish

3 tablespoons granulated sugar

1 tablespoon Worcestershire
   (page 145 or store-bought)

1 tablespoon molasses

½ cup vodka

2 cups water

1 Heat a saucepot over medium heat and add the olive oil. Add the onion and celery and season with a pinch of salt and pepper. Cook until softened and translucent, about 3 to 5 minutes.

2 Add the garlic and ginger and cook until fragrant, about 1 minute, stirring to incorporate.

3 Add the celery seed, allspice, clove, tomato paste, jalapeños and their liquid, horseradish, sugar, Worcestershire, and molasses. Stir to coat. Add a generous pinch of salt and pepper. Cook until fragrant, about 1 to 2 minutes, stirring constantly and lowering the heat if necessary to prevent scorching.

4 Add the vodka and ½ cup of water and bring to a boil, then lower the heat and simmer for at least 30 minutes and up to 90 minutes. The mixture should resemble a thinner version of tomato sauce, so add more water in ¼-cup increments as needed to thin the mixture. The longer you simmer the better, but if you're pressed for time, 30 minutes will do just fine.

5 Cool slightly, then purée in a blender until smooth. Adjust seasoning with salt and pepper, celery seed, and vodka if necessary. Bottoms up!

STORAGE NOTES: *Ketchup will keep in the refrigerator for up to one month.*

FRIED KETCHUP

YIELD: 12 pieces per cup of ketchup   START TO FINISH: 12 hours   ACTIVE TIME: 30 minutes

Hang with us. If people can deep fry ice cream and Twinkies, why the hell can't we deep fry ketchup? Move over deep-fried pickles, we've discovered the next big bar snack.

1 to 2 cups Heinz Tomato Ketchup (amount varies based upon mold)

1 cup all-purpose flour

1 cup cornstarch

2 teaspoons baking soda

3 teaspoons kosher salt, divided

1½ cups of your favorite beer (malty, lighter beers work especially well in batters)

4 cups light olive oil or canola oil, for frying

Freshly cracked black pepper, to taste

SPECIAL EQUIPMENT:

Silicone mold (we prefer rectangular "financier" style with 0.68-ounce cavities)

1 Fill each cavity of your silicone mold with ketchup. (Straight from the ketchup bottle is the most efficient way.) Place ketchup in freezer until frozen solid, about 4 hours. (Ensure ketchup is frozen solid before moving on.)

2 Make batter. Combine flour, cornstarch, baking soda, 2 teaspoons salt, and beer in a large bowl. Whisk until smooth.

3 Heat the oil to 350°F. (See our Frying Guide on page xiv.)

4 Moving quickly, remove ketchup from freezer and very carefully pop 4 pieces out of the mold. (Return the mold back to the freezer between rounds.) Dip ketchup into batter, fully coat, and carefully drop into frying oil.

5 Fry until puffed and golden, about 2 to 3 minutes. Remove from oil, place on paper towels, and immediately season to taste with remaining salt and pepper.

6 Repeat until all ketchup has been prepared. Serve as a side or on top of your burger.

STORAGE NOTES: *Eat them right away! Fried food is always a leftover let down.*

HERE'S THE SECRET to super spicy mustard: Get your hands on the freshest seeds and "open" them up by puréeing them. The smoother your purée, the stronger the flavor.

MUSTARD

The mustard aisle is quite possibly the most diverse lane in the supermarket. And for good reason—it's damn easy (and utterly addicting) to make delicious mustard. All you need are some mustard seeds and a little bit of patience. Once you nail the basic technique, there will be no stopping you. You'll bombard your friends and family with such an onslaught of beer-and-bacon-infused, red-beet-stained, spicy, whole grain mustard that they'll be begging for mercy.

We've provided you with the basics. Mustard 101, if you will. Once you master our yellow, whole grain, and Dijon mustards, you'll be on your way to bottling your own line of craft condiments.

FOOLPROOF WHOLE GRAIN MUSTARD

YIELD: 2 cups   START TO FINISH: 3 days   ACTIVE TIME: 5 minutes

What we love most about this mustard is that you can use this as the base for all other country style mustards. Add beer, wine, garlic, herbs, spices—whatever your heart desires. Simply mix your fancy mustard by hand in a bowl for a rustic approach or place all ingredients in a food processor to amplify the flavors.

⅔ cup yellow mustard seed

⅔ cup brown mustard seed

1⅓ cups distilled white vinegar

1 teaspoon kosher salt

1. Pack all ingredients into an airtight non-reactive container.

2. Store at room temperature for 3 days.

Optional: Pour contents of container into a food processor and pulse for 10 to 15 seconds, just until the seeds begin to pop open. (Or continue to blitz seeds until smooth for a spicier rendition.)

STORAGE NOTES: *Mustard will keep in the refrigerator for up to three months.*

"BURN YOUR NOSE HAIRS" YELLOW MUSTARD

YIELD: About 2 cups   START TO FINISH: 12 hours   ACTIVE TIME: 5 minutes

If you're freaks like us and love a good nostril rush, take a hard sniff off the blender after puréeing. Caution: huffing mustard may induce hallucinations.

½ cup yellow mustard seed

1¼ cups distilled white vinegar

½ cup water

2 teaspoons turmeric

2 teaspoons kosher salt

1 Soak all ingredients in an airtight non-reactive container at room temperature overnight.

2 The next day, place all ingredients in a blender and purée until smooth, about 3 to 5 minutes.

STORAGE NOTES: *Mustard will keep in the refrigerator for up to three months.*

DIJON

YIELD: About 2 cups   START TO FINISH: 12 hours   ACTIVE TIME: 5 minutes

Here's a fun fact: In Europe, Grey Poupon is spicy as hell. Stateside, it's dulled down to accommodate the average American palate. Dijon isn't just zippy; it also has a refined profile and depth, which is a result of the white wine vinegar, white wine, and the combination of both yellow and brown mustard seeds. The brown seeds provide this quintessential mustard with that earthy, nutty flavor.

¼ cup yellow mustard seed

¼ cup brown mustard seed

1¼ cups white wine vinegar

½ cup white wine

2 teaspoons kosher salt

1 Soak all ingredients in an airtight non-reactive container at room temperature overnight.

2 The next day, place all ingredients in blender and purée until smooth, approximately 3 to 5 minutes.

3 Pack it back up in an airtight container and spread it on anything and everything.

STORAGE NOTES: *Mustard will keep in the refrigerator for up to three months.*

BACON & BEER HONEY MUSTARD

YIELD: About 2 cups   START TO FINISH: 5 minutes

Bacon, beer, and mustard go together, well, like bacon, beer, and mustard. This mustard is awesome spread on a burger, as a dip for your pretzel, or just eaten with a spoon. We won't judge.

¼ cup amber ale

6 strips of cooked bacon, ¼ cup of fat reserved

¼ cup honey

½ cup Foolproof Whole Grain Mustard
   (page 127 or store-bought)

1 teaspoon kosher salt

¼ cup Standard Mayo (page 133 or store-bought)

1 Purée ale, bacon, bacon fat, honey, mustard, and salt in blender until smooth.

2 Pour into a bowl and whisk in mayo. Refrigerate until cold.

STORAGE NOTES: *Mustard will keep in the refrigerator for up to two weeks.*

POLISH BEET MUSTARD

YIELD: About 2 to 3 cups   START TO FINISH: 1½ hours   ACTIVE TIME: 15 minutes

Richard's dad, born in Poland, is no stranger to caraway, dill, and horseradish—the holy trinity of Polish cooking. For this mustard, we added roasted beets to create the ultimate Polish spread. It's burger-ready and Chudy-approved. Polish accent recommended but not required.

1 medium-sized beet

1 tablespoon caraway seeds

1 cup mustard (any of our homemade or store-bought)

¼ cup fresh dill, chopped

2 tablespoons fresh horseradish, peeled and grated

1. Preheat the oven to 325°F. Wrap the beet in aluminum foil and roast until soft, about 60 to 75 minutes. Peel the beet when cool enough to handle.

2. Dry roast caraway seeds in a small skillet over low heat until fragrant, about 3 to 4 minutes.

3. Combine everything in a blender and give it a whirl until smooth, adding a touch of water if the mixture is too thick. Breathe it in if you have any sinuses you want to clear up.

4. Slather it on a burger, kielbasa, or pierogi of your choice.

STORAGE NOTES: *Mustard will keep in the refrigerator for up to two weeks.*

MAYO

Here is everything you always wanted to know about making homemade mayo but were afraid to try. Trust us when we tell you that you'll taste the difference between store-bought and homemade mayo instantly, making you a convert for life.

....

STANDARD MAYO

YIELD: 2 cups   START TO FINISH: 5 minutes

Making mayo means creating an emulsion. Don't go too slow; don't go too fast. Both can cause your emulsion to break. Picture Italian dressing before you shake the bottle. Everything is separated. Vinaigrettes tend to be temporary emulsions, while mayonnaise is a permanent emulsion (which is why it's so thick and creamy). A good pace for streaming oil is about thirty seconds per cup.

If you do happen to break your mayo, all is not lost. Simply place all ingredients into a container with a pour spout, add two new yolks to the processor along with one newly measured tablespoon of ground mustard and one newly measured tablespoon of lemon juice, and begin the process again, this time using your broken mayo in place of oil. Your mayo may be a little tangier than usual, but we'd rather have you do that than throw everything away and start all over. Plus, repeating these steps will help you get better at creating an emulsion.

2 egg yolks

1½ teaspoons kosher salt

1 tablespoon ground mustard

3 tablespoons lemon juice

2 cups light olive oil

1 teaspoon cold water

1   Place yolks, salt, mustard, and lemon juice in food processor and mix for 30 seconds.

2   With machine still on, pour half the oil into the processor in a slow, steady stream.

3   Add cold water.

4   Slowly and steadily stream in the remaining cup of oil. (Keep in mind that steps 2 through 4 should take about 60 seconds total.)

5   Transfer to a container for storage.

STORAGE NOTES: *Mayo will keep in the refrigerator until the expiration date of the eggs you used.*

MISO CURRY MAYO

YIELD: 2½ cups   START TO FINISH: 5 minutes

4 tablespoons canned
   red curry paste

2 teaspoons ground yellow
   mustard seed

½ teaspoon kosher salt

2 teaspoons soy sauce

2 teaspoons your favorite
   fish sauce

2 teaspoons red miso

3 tablespoons lime juice

2 egg yolks

2 cups light olive oil or canola oil

1 teaspoon cold water

1 Place all ingredients except for oil and water in food processor and mix for 30 seconds.

2 With the machine still running, pour half the oil into the processor in a slow, steady stream.

3 Add cold water.

4 Slowly and steadily stream in the remaining cup of oil. (Keep in mind that steps 2 through 4 should take about 60 seconds total.)

5 Refrigerate until ready to use.

STORAGE NOTES: *Mayo will keep in the refrigerator until the expiration date of the eggs you used.*

CREOLE MAYO

YIELD: 3 cups   START TO FINISH: 5 to 10 minutes

This is an heirloom recipe. This sauce was something Sammy's father, Big Sam, used to prepare at his family's neighborhood bar and grill in Chapel Hill. The chopped hard-boiled eggs are representative of an older era in American cookery, one of deep Southern heritage and methods. Folks today may not be accustomed to hard-boiled eggs in their cold sauces, but try this mayo and you'll see why we're glad this old technique lives on.

2 cups Standard Mayo (page 133 or store-bought)

3 tablespoons Bourbon Barrel Red Hot (page 142 or Tabasco)

1 teaspoon granulated sugar

¼ teaspoon kosher salt

2 garlic cloves, minced

⅓ cup Foolproof Whole Grain Mustard (page 127 or store-bought)

⅓ cup horseradish, freshly grated

¼ bunch parsley, finely chopped

2 hard-boiled eggs, cooled and grated or finely chopped

1 Place all ingredients in a large bowl and mix well. Serve or refrigerate immediately.

STORAGE NOTES: Mayo will keep in the refrigerator until the expiration date of the eggs you used.

RED REMOULADE

YIELD: 2½ cups   START TO FINISH: 5 minutes

In Louisiana, they like to add dried chiles and ketchup to their remoulade, giving this sauce that quintessential red hue and tangy, smoky depth. Down on the Gulf Coast, they serve it alongside shrimp and other deep-fried fish, but we love it on a burger topped with some Johnnycake Fried Oysters, Pan Fried Pickled Green Tomatoes, and Pop's Dirty Slaw.

2 cups Standard Mayo (page 133 or store-bought)

1 teaspoon Worcestershire (page 145 or store-bought)

2 tablespoons Foolproof Whole Grain Mustard (page 127 or store-bought)

2 tablespoons Umami Ketchup (page 119 or Heinz)

1 teaspoon cayenne

1 tablespoon lemon juice

2 teaspoons prepared horseradish

1 tablespoon minced garlic

1 teaspoon celery salt

1 teaspoon smoked paprika

1. Whisk all ingredients together. Serve or refrigerate immediately.

STORAGE NOTES: *Mayo will keep in the refrigerator until the expiration date of the eggs you used.*

FLORIBBEAN TARTAR

YIELD: 2½ cups   START TO FINISH: 12 hours   ACTIVE TIME: 5 minutes

When we fantasize about white sandy beaches and the aroma of wild-caught fish roasting over hardwood charcoal, we don't lust for a one-night-stand, run-of-the-mill tartar sauce. We want the flavors to measure up to our sensual surroundings. This sauce takes the idea of a traditional tartar and renders it burger-worthy by kicking it up a notch—just like the great Emeril Lagasse. *Bam!* If you really want to get that true-grit Floridian flavor, season your burger with Old Bay. Oh yeah, baby.

1 extremely ripe mango

1 scotch bonnet (wear gloves when handling—or else!)

¼ cup guava nectar

2 fresh kaffir lime leaves

¼ teaspoon pure vanilla extract

2 cups Standard Mayo (page 133 or store-bought)

½ red onion, cut into a small dice

½ sweet bell pepper (your favorite color), cut into a small dice

½ teaspoon kosher salt

½ teaspoon ground cinnamon

½ teaspoon ground cumin

¼ teaspoon ground allspice

1 Peel and scoop out the flesh of the mango and place in a blender. Squeeze the flesh of the pit over blender and extract as much juice as you can.

2 Add scotch bonnet, guava nectar, kaffir lime leaves, and vanilla extract, and purée until smooth.

3 Pour into a bowl with all remaining ingredients and whisk until evenly mixed.

4 Refrigerate overnight. (This will allow the sauce to thicken and the flavors to marry.)

STORAGE NOTES: *Mayo will keep in the refrigerator until the expiration date of the eggs you used.*

BBQ SAUCE

Man has probably aspired to perfect the art of barbecue since the discovery of fire. This fascinates us. We love the idea of digging a large ditch, burning hardwood to a smoldering coal, gracefully wrapping an entire animal in banana leaves as a gift to Mother Earth, and devouring the spoils of a day's worth of attentive cooking.

We admire all that is barbecue and believe those who do it well are proof of human evolution. In this section, we travel down US Route 61, I-40, I-85, and countless country back roads as we share some of our all-time favorite variations of regional American barbecue sauces. They deserve—and need—to go on your burger.

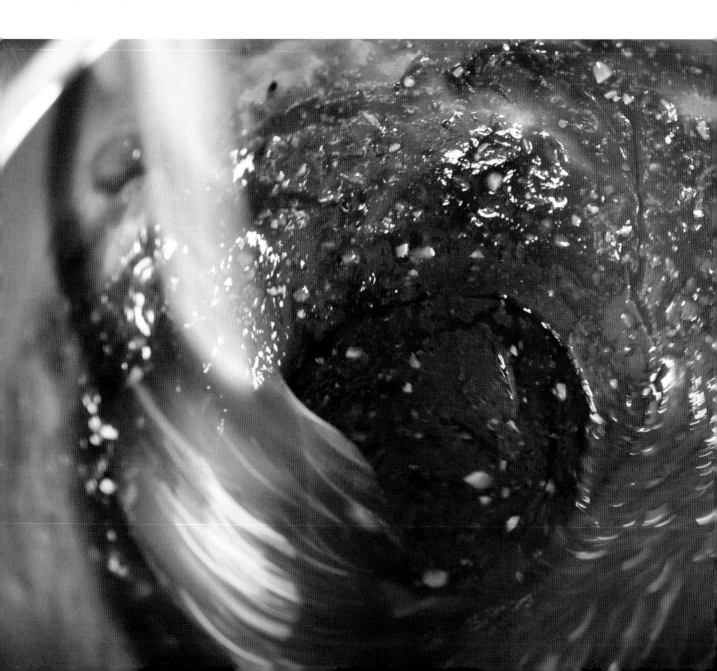

KC PIT MASTER

YIELD: 3 cups   START TO FINISH: About 4 hours   ACTIVE TIME: 30 to 45 minutes

Kansas City barbecue is known for its wide variety of meats, including pork, brisket, and ribs—but the sauce is the signature ingredient. Typically, the meat is seasoned with a dry rub before it is smoked, and the sauce is served tableside. KC sauces are tomatoey, rich, and often sweetened with molasses. Some are heavy on the sweet while others lean toward the spicy side, and most have a smoky element. The smokiness is what truly distinguishes it from other ketchupy sauces. It's not uncommon for there to be several varieties available, including extra sweet, extra fiery, and pit master.

When making this sauce, don't skimp on the spices and beer. The ancho and chipotle are critical to creating a smoky depth. If you can't get your hands on Dark Horse Black Ale, find a comparable Schwarzbier. Mounting this sauce with a rich craft beer ties the various flavors of sweet, spicy, tangy, and smoky together into a unique, complex profile that will elevate your burger to unfathomable heights.

1 small yellow onion, diced

1 jalapeño, minced

3 garlic cloves, minced

1 teaspoon plus a pinch kosher salt

2 tablespoons light olive oil or canola oil

¼ cup brown sugar

¼ cup molasses

¼ cup distilled white vinegar

2 tablespoons Worcestershire (page 145 or store-bought)

2 cups Umami Ketchup (page 119 or Heinz)

1 teaspoon ground chipotle

1 teaspoon ground ancho chile

1 tablespoon freshly cracked black pepper

1 teaspoon freshly cracked white peppercorn

½ cup Dark Horse Black Ale (or comparable Schwarzbier black lager beer)

1. In a saucepot over medium heat, sweat onion, jalapeño, and garlic with a pinch of salt in canola oil until softened, about 7 to 10 minutes.

2. Add brown sugar, molasses, vinegar, Worcestershire, ketchup, ground chipotle and ancho chile, 1 teaspoon salt, and both black and white pepper. Simmer for 30 minutes.

3. Remove from heat. Using a stick blender or upright blender, and being careful not to burn the living shit out of yourself, slowly pour the beer into the sauce then purée until smooth.

4. Place over extremely low flame and barely simmer for 3 hours, stirring occasionally to make sure the mixture doesn't burn or stick to the bottom of the pot. Adjust seasoning with salt and pepper if needed. Cool completely before storing in the refrigerator.

STORAGE NOTES: This sauce will keep in a covered container for up to three weeks. Freeze unused sauce for up to two months.

CAROLINA GOLD

YIELD: 1¼ cups   START TO FINISH: 10 minutes

While there are three regionally distinct barbecue styles offered across the fine state of South Carolina, the chosen sauce of the midlands, Carolina Gold, is by far the most unique.

What sets Carolina Gold apart is its tangy mustard base complemented by a deep, rich sweetness from honey, molasses, and brown sugar, along with a kick of smoke and capsaicin (which is the element in peppers that makes them hot). Even though it's usually paired with pork, you won't find a single Carolinian balking when you slather it all over your next beefy burger.

1 cup "Burn Your Nose Hairs" Yellow Mustard (page 128 or store-bought)

¼ cup honey

1 tablespoon light brown sugar

¼ cup molasses

1 tablespoon Bourbon Barrel Red Hot (page 142 or Tabasco)

½ tablespoon Worcestershire (page 145 or store-bought)

½ teaspoon liquid smoke

1½ tablespoons kosher salt

1½ tablespoons freshly cracked black pepper

① Combine all ingredients in a blender and buzz it up until completely smooth, about 2 minutes. Taste and adjust seasoning if needed.

② How you use this kickass sauce it up to you. Use it as a wet seasoning (see *Spice the Nation*, chapter 2), baste your burger in it as it cooks, or straight up spread it like a condiment on your finished patty. You can't go wrong with the Gold.

STORAGE NOTES: *Sauce will keep in the refrigerator for up to three weeks.*

LIQUID SMOKE is exactly what it sounds like. Smoke, generated from delicious hardwood, transformed into a liquid by means of combustion chambers and condensers. Yeah, pretty manly shit. A little goes a long way, so use sparingly. You can pick up a bottle at your grocery store or online.

LUAU GLAZE

YIELD: About 3 cups   START TO FINISH: 1½ hours   ACTIVE TIME: 30 minutes

Ah, the luau: Hawaii's tropical smorgasbord that features a whole suckling pig, traditionally cooked kālua style. Samoans have cooked their pigs in this manner for roughly 3,500 years, when the first voyagers from Southeast Asia are believed to have arrived in Polynesia. Crunchy, salty skin, melt-in-your-mouth, drip-down-your-chin fat, and tender, smoky meat. What more could you want?

Nothing really, but if you're at a luau nowadays, you'll definitely come across this Hawaiian BBQ condiment, which tastes amazing on a burger. We developed this sauce to pay homage to the history, traditions, and flavors of the wonderful people throughout the Hawaiian Islands. Mahalo and aloha!

2 tablespoons light olive oil
or canola oil

1 small yellow onion, diced

8 cloves garlic, sliced
⅛-inch thick

1 jalapeño, sliced ⅛-inch thick

2 cups Umami Ketchup (page 119
or Heinz)

¾ cup soy sauce

¾ cup pineapple juice

¼ cup rice wine vinegar

¼ cup brown sugar

2-inch chunk ginger, peeled
and sliced ⅛-inch thick

1 In a large saucepot over medium heat, sweat onion, garlic, and jalapeño in the oil until translucent, about 7 to 10 minutes.

2 Add ketchup, soy sauce, pineapple juice, vinegar, and brown sugar.

3 Bring to gentle simmer and cook on low for 1 hour, stirring occasionally to avoid burning or sticking.

4 Pour into a blender along with fresh ginger, and being careful not to burn the living shit out of yourself, purée until smooth.

5 We'll look the other way if you want to make chicken teriyaki with this sauce, but don't be a schlub: it's meant for your burger, whether it's a wet seasoning (see *Spice the Nation*, chapter 2), a baste, or a condiment.

STORAGE NOTES: *Glaze will keep covered in the refrigerator for up to two weeks.*

BOURBON BARREL RED HOT

YIELD: About 3 cups   START TO FINISH: 8 days   ACTIVE TIME: 1 hour

Tabasco is one of our favorite types of hot sauce. It's made with only three ingredients—distilled vinegar, red pepper, and salt—and aged in American whiskey barrels for up to three years, which gives the sauce that distinct woody, complex flavor profile.

The Tabasco process inspired this recipe, but obviously we can't age our hot sauce in a 53-gallon bourbon barrel like they do. Plus, we think using chips is rather genius! This little trick imparts flavor faster than traditional barrel aging. Don't be put off by the wood chips—you're simply infusing the hot sauce with toasted oak and robust bourbon.

2 cups distilled white vinegar

2 cups water

3 tablespoons kosher salt

1½ tablespoons granulated sugar

½ cup garlic cloves

½ heaping cup dried chile de arbol

½ teaspoon ground chipotle

½ teaspoon ground habanero

⅛ teaspoon xanthan gum (available online or well-stocked grocery stores)

SPECIAL EQUIPMENT:

1 heaping cup Jim Beam bourbon barrel wood chips

1 Place all ingredients except xanthan gum and wood chips into a saucepot and bring to a gentle simmer.

2 Place lid on pot, simmer very gently for 5 minutes, turn off heat, and allow to steep for 1 hour.

3 Bring back up to a gentle simmer and cook for 60 seconds. Turn off heat, place lid on tightly, and steep for another hour.

4 Pour into blender (you may have to do this is two batches), and being careful not to burn the living shit out of yourself, purée until as smooth as possible.

5 Pass through a fine mesh sieve and pour back into a clean blender.

6 Turn blender on medium speed and slowly shear in the xanthan gum. Blend for 60 seconds to ensure all xanthan has been activated. Refrigerate overnight.

7 Pass sauce through a fine mesh sieve once more to pull out any clumped xanthan and excess pulp.

8 Rinse wood chips under hot water to remove any surface dirt.

9 Place wood chips and hot sauce in an airtight non-reactive container. Shake for 60 seconds.

10 Allow sauce to age at room temperature for 7 days. Pour the hot sauce through a fine mesh sieve to strain out the wood chips and any small particles. Use in place of your favorite hot sauce, you filthy animal.

STORAGE NOTES: *Sauce will keep in the refrigerator for at least two months.*

....

SHEAR is a term often used to describe the technique of adding a hydrocolloid to a liquid. To shear, place your hydrocolloid (in this case xanthan) on a spoon and slowly stream a steady dusting of granules into the liquid while it is being blended.

....

ALABAMA WHITE

YIELD: 1¼ cups   START TO FINISH: 10 minutes

We love mayonnaise, but them folks down in Alabama take it to the next level of devotion. Upon pulling chicken from the barby, they toss that bird straight into a bowl full of sauce and smother it like they're making hot wings. Except instead of buffalo sauce, they use mayo. And it's really freaking good. When using this sauce on your burger, do it like you're down in the derrty and coat your entire burger in this decadence. Trust us, it's magic.

1 cup Standard Mayo (page 133 or store-bought)

2 tablespoons Foolproof Whole Grain Mustard (page 127 or store-bought)

1-inch chunk fresh horseradish, peeled and finely grated

1 tablespoon garlic, minced

2 tablespoons apple cider vinegar

¼ teaspoon kosher salt

½ teaspoon granulated sugar

2 teaspoons freshly cracked black pepper

1 Mix all ingredients together in a large bowl.

2 Resist drinking it and slather all over your burger.

STORAGE NOTES: *Sauce will keep in the refrigerator until the expiration date of the eggs you used.*

THE REFRIGERATOR DOOR

We keep our refrigerator doors packed to the Plexiglas with chip dip, steak sauce, and a fine assortment of hot sauces. The myriad choices inevitably include sriracha (because at this point, we think we can all acknowledge the ubiquitous presence of the rooster), ketchup-mustard-mayo hybrids, and stealthy umami bombs. The sound of gyrating glass jars gets more melodic each time we open the door as our collection of homemade sauces grows. Yes, all those bottles make putting away a twelve-pack challenging, but they are worth it. These sauces are a man's best friend and go great with almost everything, like pizza, chops, wings, nachos, and oh yeah, burgers!

WORCESTERSHIRE

YIELD: 2 cups   START TO FINISH: 1 hour

This is a *sauce* (not a runny, bottled mess), and it should be treated as such. It has a lovely viscosity that you'll find plenty of uses for. Don't let the long list of ingredients scare you off—just dump everything into the pot and simmer away.

2 tablespoons olive oil

½ cup onion (red or white), diced

4 cloves garlic, minced

½-inch piece fresh ginger, peeled and minced

Pinch crushed red pepper flakes

½ teaspoon ground cinnamon

4 to 6 whole cloves, or ½ teaspoon ground clove

2 to 3 whole cardamom pods, or ¼ teaspoon ground cardamom

2 to 3 whole allspice berries, or ½ teaspoon ground allspice

¼ cup molasses, preferably blackstrap

½ cup white wine vinegar

¼ cup malt vinegar

¼ cup balsamic vinegar

3 tablespoons Maggi seasoning or light soy sauce

¼ cup fish sauce or 5 olive oil-packed anchovies, finely chopped into a paste

⅛ cup tamarind paste (found in Asian markets or well-stocked grocery stores)

⅔ cup granulated sugar

Kosher salt, to taste

① Heat oil in a saucepot over medium heat. Add the onion and cook until soft and translucent, about 5 to 7 minutes.

② Add the garlic and ginger and cook until aromatic, about 1 minute.

③ Add the red pepper flakes, cinnamon, clove, cardamom, and allspice and stir to incorporate with the onion and garlic until fragrant, about 30 seconds.

④ Add the remaining ingredients and stir to coat.

⑤ Once the mixture starts bubbling lightly, turn the heat down very low and simmer for at least 30 minutes and up to 1 hour. Simmering for 30 minutes will do the trick, but if you want more intense flavors, simmer longer. Thin with water as you go if the mixture starts to thicken or boil too rapidly.

⑥ Cool slightly, then purée in a blender until smooth, seasoning with salt if necessary. This sauce is quite thick; if you want it thinner, simply add water as needed and blend to combine.

⑦ Enjoy this sauce right away, or refrigerate it for a few days to let the flavors marry.

STORAGE NOTES: *Sauce will keep in the refrigerator for several months.*

STEAK SAUCE

YIELD: 2½ cups   START TO FINISH: 1¾ hours   ACTIVE TIME: 25 minutes

Ditch the A-1 and give this fresh steak sauce a try. Popping with orange and raisins and backed by black garlic and vinegar, it straddles that delicious line between steak and BBQ sauce.

2 teaspoons canola oil

1 small onion, chopped

2 cloves black garlic, chopped (or substitute 2 cloves fresh garlic)

⅓ cup sherry vinegar

¼ cup raisins

¼ cup molasses

1 tablespoon Worcestershire (page 145 or store-bought)

2 tablespoons Dijon (page 128 or store-bought)

Zest of 1 orange

1 bay leaf

2 cups Umami Ketchup (page 119 or Heinz)

¼ teaspoon crushed red pepper flakes

¼ teaspoon coriander seeds

1. Heat oil in a medium saucepan, add the onion and garlic, and cook until lightly browned, about 5 to 7 minutes.

2. Add the vinegar and cook until it reduces by half, about 7 to 10 minutes.

3. Add the remaining ingredients and cook over very low heat, 60 to 90 minutes, stirring every now and then and adding water periodically to thin and to prevent scorching and sticking.

4. Cool slightly; remove bay leaf and purée in a blender until smooth.

STORAGE NOTES: *Sauce will keep in the refrigerator for up to two weeks.*

JALAPEÑO HOT SAUCE

YIELD: 3 cups   START TO FINISH: 3½ days   ACTIVE TIME: 10 minutes

The key to making a kickin' hot sauce is finding the perfect balance of capsaicin (that fiery element of peppers), acidity, salinity, and sweetness. Depending on the spiciness of your peppers or your own preference, you can omit the habanero or add a few more. Once you're comfortable with this process, this recipe is a great template for your inevitable hot sauce experiments. (And remember: wear those gloves when handling the scotch bonnet, or you'll be sorry!)

1 pound jalapeños, thinly sliced

1 habanero or scotch bonnet, split in half

⅓ cup granulated sugar

6 tablespoons kosher salt

1¼ cups distilled white vinegar

1¼ cups water

¼ teaspoon xanthan gum

1. Place all ingredients except for xanthan gum in a non-reactive airtight container and steep at room temperature for 3 days.

2. Purée in a blender until as smooth as possible.

3. Pass through a fine mesh sieve and pour back into clean blender.

4. Turn blender to medium speed and slowly shear in the xanthan gum. Blend for 60 seconds to ensure all xanthan has been activated. Refrigerate overnight.

5. Pass sauce through a fine mesh sieve once more to pull out any clumped xanthan and excess pulp.

STORAGE NOTES: *Sauce will keep in the refrigerator for up to one month.*

RED ROOSTER

YIELD: About 2 cups   START TO FINISH: 5 days   ACTIVE TIME: 25 minutes

This is a condiment you could easily just buy, but c'mon, where's the fun in that? Our sriracha ferments for a few days, adding layer upon layer of flavor. We suggest using gloves when chopping the chiles, otherwise we can't be held responsible for what, where, and whom you touch afterwards. Warning: may cause extreme homemade sriracha addiction.

1½ pounds fresh Fresno chiles, stems removed

4 garlic cloves, peeled and smashed with the back of a knife

¼ cup brown sugar

2 tablespoons kosher salt

½ cup distilled white vinegar

1 Using gloves, cut the chiles in half. Scoop out the seeds and ribs of about half of the chiles. (Most of the heat lies in these elements, so scoop out more or less depending on your preference.)

2 In a food processor, pulse the chiles, garlic, sugar, and salt until everything is coarsely chopped. Scoop the mixture out and place in a large mason jar. Seal and keep in a cool, dark place and out of direct sunlight for about 5 days, or until small bubbles start appearing on the sides and surface. Shake the jar daily.

3 After 5 days, purée the contents in a blender with the vinegar until smooth, about 1 minute. Don't inhale those fumes, that shit is hot! If the sauce is not completely smooth, strain it.

4 In a small saucepan, heat over medium-low heat. Lower the heat if sauce begins to bubble too rapidly, and cook until the sauce starts to thicken and coats the back of a spoon, about 15 to 20 minutes. (The sauce will thicken as it cools so don't reduce it too much.)

5 Seal it back up in a mason jar or squeeze bottle and refrigerate until ready to use.

STORAGE NOTES: *Sauce will keep in the refrigerator for up to one month.*

MARK'S ILL DIP

YIELD: About 3 cups   START TO FINISH: 12 hours   ACTIVE TIME: 20 minutes

Our close friend chef Mark O'Leary has the ability to season to perfection, which is why we had to share his hell-of-a-good dip with y'all.

Marky says, "Use it for chips, pita, celery, carrots, chicken wings, your finger, mozzarella sticks, double cheeseburgers, whatever! You'll never be stuck picking Lipton's dried onions out of your teeth during football again."

2 cups sour cream

½ cup bacon (approximately 4 slices), cooked and roughly chopped

¾ teaspoon kosher salt

½ teaspoon freshly cracked black pepper

3¾ teaspoons onion powder

3¾ teaspoons garlic powder

¼ lime, juice and zest

1 tablespoon plus 1½ teaspoons Bourbon Barrel Red Hot (page 142 or Tabasco)

¼ bunch scallions, thinly sliced

1 Mix all ingredients together in a large bowl.

2 Refrigerate overnight for tastiest results. Use as a dip for chips, a spread for your favorite burger, or just eat it like O'Leary: with a spoon in your underwear.

STORAGE NOTES: *Dip will keep in the refrigerator for up to one week.*

POP'S RUSSIAN

YIELD: 2 cups   START TO FINISH: 12 hours   ACTIVE TIME: 5 minutes

All imitators beware: there is only one true Pop's Russian. This recipe has roots from Sammy's father, Big Sam, and has been in the family since the 1950s. Yeah, it's worth hanging on to.

Classically, it's prepared with Heinz Chili Sauce. If you use ketchup and try to call it Pop's, the old man will slap you upside the head with a shoe. But seriously, make this Russian and everyone will love it and you. It's the stuff with which award-winning burgers are made.

½ medium yellow onion

½ green bell pepper

1 cup Standard Mayo (page 133 or store-bought)

½ cup Heinz Chili Sauce, no exceptions

½ teaspoon granulated sugar

½ teaspoon kosher salt

1 teaspoon freshly cracked black pepper

2 dashes Lea & Perrins Worcestershire Sauce (Pops uses Lea & Perrins; we want to keep this recipe authentic!)

1 Finely mince onion and green pepper in a food processor. We prefer to use the pulse button here to ensure we don't create a purée but rather a finely minced product with a bit of crunch and texture.

2 Combine all ingredients in a large bowl, mix well, and refrigerate immediately. Allow flavors to marry under refrigeration for at least 12 hours before use.

3 Pour this all over your burgers and wait for people to bow at your feet.

STORAGE NOTES: *Dressing will keep in the refrigerator for up to one week.*

CHECK OUT POP'S RUSSIAN IN ACTION!
Turn the page! →

THE McMAYOR

Double Stack

IPA SESAME SEED BUN
Page 38

POP'S RUSSIAN
Page 151

Kosher Dill CHIPS
Page 171

CARAMELIZED ONIONS

CHEDDAR CHEESE

SECRET STASH

Look on the top shelf of the fridge, behind the sour cream, yogurt, herbs, and leftover casserole. That's where you'll find the secret stash. Various pint containers filled with savory marmalades, smooth legume spreads, compound butters, numerous vegetable numbers, and of course, repurposed junk food. It's basically the Area 51 of our refrigerators, and up until now, these unidentified spreadable products have remained classified.

....

RED ONION MARMALADE

YIELD: 1 cup   START TO FINISH: 1 hour   ACTIVE TIME: 20 minutes

2 red onions, thinly sliced

2 tablespoons light olive oil
or canola oil

¼ cup granulated sugar

¼ cup fruity red wine

1 teaspoon kosher salt

1 teaspoon freshly cracked
black pepper

2 teaspoons fresh thyme,
finely chopped

1 In a saucepot over medium heat, slowly caramelize the onions with oil for about 20 minutes, stirring occasionally.

2 Add remainder of ingredients and simmer until red wine has reduced into a syrupy liquid and color of onions is a deep, dark purple, about 25 to 30 minutes.

3 Spread onion mixture on a sheet tray to cool.

4 Store in a bowl or plastic container and refrigerate until ready to use.

STORAGE NOTES: *Marmalade will keep in the refrigerator for up to two weeks.*

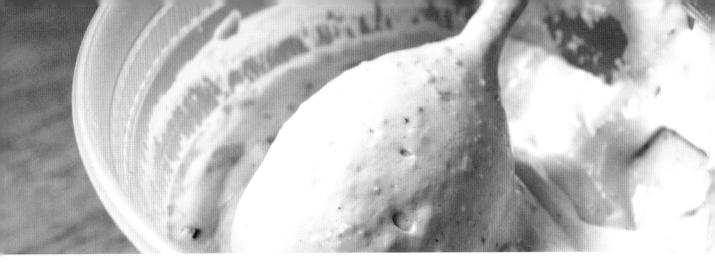

AVOCADO RANCH

YIELD: 2 cups   START TO FINISH: 5 minutes

We love avocados as much as the next girl, but sometimes simply slicing them and throwing them on top of a burger won't cut it. Now, mixing it with sour cream, buttermilk, and the beloved flavors of the hidden valley? That's culinary gold, baby.

1 ripe avocado

¾ cup sour cream

1½ tablespoons lemon juice

2 teaspoons red wine vinegar

2 teaspoons Worcestershire
    (page 145 or store-bought)

2 garlic cloves, minced

½ teaspoon celery seed

1½ teaspoons kosher salt

1½ teaspoons freshly cracked
    black pepper

¼ cup buttermilk

1   Combine all ingredients except buttermilk in food processor and purée until silky smooth.

2   Pour into a large bowl and whisk in buttermilk.

3   Refrigerate until cold.

STORAGE NOTES: *This dressing is best enjoyed within two days.*

CHARRED GREEN CHILE BUTTER

YIELD: 1 cup   START TO FINISH: 3½ hours   ACTIVE TIME: 30 minutes

A dab of this sharp green chile butter is just what the doctor ordered. Add it to your burger just moments before it comes off the grill and watch as the butter melts right into that bad boy. Talk about sexy time, my friend.

1 pasilla chile pepper

1 anaheim chile pepper

1 poblano chile pepper

2 teaspoons light olive oil

1½ teaspoons kosher salt, divided

½ teaspoon freshly cracked black pepper, plus more to taste

½ pound unsalted butter, room temperature

1   Remove stems and lightly season chiles with light olive oil, a pinch of salt, and pepper. Char on grill until evenly colored all over.

2   Place in a plastic container with a few splashes of hot water and press lid on tight. Rest for 10 minutes. Peel skin and remove seeds.

3   Purée chiles in blender.

4   Pour into stand mixer with ½ teaspoon of salt, ½ teaspoon of pepper, and butter and whip with paddle until fully incorporated and fluffy, about 2 to 4 minutes. (This step can also be done with a hand-held mixer or by hand with a little bit of elbow grease.)

5   Using a rubber spatula, transfer butter onto plastic wrap and roll into a log. Refrigerate until solid, about 3 hours.

6   Once firm, unwrap butter and slice off a big, fat coin. Place onto your burger before it comes off the grill or griddle. (Allowing your slice of butter to soften at room temperature for 15 minutes will help it melt evenly on your burger.)

STORAGE NOTES: *Butter will keep in the refrigerator for up to two weeks and in the freezer for up to three months.*

"COOL RANCH" RANCH

YIELD: About 2 cups   START TO FINISH: 25 minutes

To ensure your sauce comes out rich and creamy, allow the blender to run for four to five minutes. It seems extreme, but this intense friction will cause the mixture to heat, breaking down the chips and releasing the natural cornstarch, which acts as a thickener. If you don't blend long enough, the sauce will be grainy and loose. Make your friends guess what the secret ingredient is; it'll blow their silly little minds.

1 snack size bag Doritos Cool Ranch Tortilla Chips, crushed

1¼ cups buttermilk

1 teaspoon kosher salt

1 teaspoon freshly cracked black pepper

1 tablespoon lemon juice

1 Soak crushed Doritos in buttermilk in a food-strength blender (or Vitamix) for 20 minutes.

2 Add the rest of the ingredients and purée in blender until thick, creamy, and smooth, about 4 to 5 minutes.

3 Chill until ready to use. It's best served cold from the refrigerator.

STORAGE NOTES: Ranch will keep in the refrigerator for up to two weeks.

CREAMY CHIMICHURRI

YIELD: 3 cups   START TO FINISH: 3 hours   ACTIVE TIME: 5 minutes

Classic Argentinian Chimichurri is made with parsley, but we can't get enough cilantro in our lives. We developed this particular variation on chimichurri to be very potent, sort of like a concentrate, so that when you whisk it into sour cream and mayo you can still enjoy its personality.

3 limes, zest and juice

½ bunch cilantro, stems and leaves

1 tablespoon ground coriander

1 tablespoon ground cumin

2 garlic cloves, minced

2 cups sour cream

1 cup Standard Mayo (page 133 or store-bought)

1½ teaspoons kosher salt

1 teaspoon freshly cracked black pepper

1 Place lime zest and juice, cilantro, coriander, cumin, and garlic in a food processor and purée until smooth but still textured. Congratulations! You have now created a concentrated chimichurri.

2 Place the mixture in a bowl, add the sour cream and mayo, and whisk until thoroughly incorporated.

3 Season with salt and pepper and refrigerate for at least 3 hours before eating so that flavors can marry.

STORAGE NOTES: *Sauce will keep in the refrigerator for up to two weeks.*

CAMOTES AL HORNO CREMA

YIELD: 3 cups   START TO FINISH: 3 hours   ACTIVE TIME: 30 minutes

Camotes al horno is one of our favorite Mexican dishes. Hailing from Puebla, this dish traditionally consists of yams roasted with honey, sugar, and butter. Sweet and creamy, this succulent side complements charred lean beef the way applesauce accompanies a pork chop.

Our sincere love for this pairing serves as the inspiration for this burger condiment. We bolster the spice profile and balance the sweetness with some lime. This recipe is super simple; keep that little secret (and any leftovers) to yourself.

1 pound sweet potatoes, scrubbed

¾ cup sour cream

1¾ teaspoons kosher salt

½ teaspoon cinnamon

½ teaspoon freshly cracked black pepper

1 teaspoon ground ancho chile

2 teaspoons lime juice

Zest of ½ lime

1 Roast sweet potatoes whole and unpeeled at 300°F until a clear sugary liquid starts to ooze out of them, about 75 to 90 minutes.

2 Cool potatoes for 30 minutes before handling and peel the skin off.

3 Purée sweet potatoes in a food processor until smooth, adding a couple drops of water or oil if needed.

4 In a medium bowl, combine sweet potatoes with the remaining ingredients. Whisk until mixed thoroughly and chill. (The crema will turn out creamier if whisked together as opposed to puréed in a food processor. Its luscious body is worth the extra bowl.)

STORAGE NOTES: *Crema will keep in the refrigerator for at least one week.*

GARLICKY RED BEAN SPREAD

YIELD: About 3 cups   START TO FINISH: 14 to 16 hours   ACTIVE TIME: 20 to 30 minutes

If you've never used dry beans before, this is your chance. Canned beans work in a pinch but nothing beats the natural creaminess of dry beans. Add the Spreadable Garlic into the mix and we guarantee you'll be talking about this spread for months.

½ cup dry kidney beans

2 cups water

¼ cup dry white wine (grüner veltliner is a good bet)

1 bay leaf

1 teaspoon freshly cracked black pepper, plus more to taste

1½ teaspoons kosher salt, plus more to taste

1½ teaspoons lemon juice

2 tablespoons extra virgin olive oil

1 teaspoon NOLA Smoky Andouille (page 30)

½ cup Spreadable Garlic (page 218)

1. Soak beans overnight.

2. Rinse beans and place in pot with 2 cups of fresh water, wine, bay leaf, black pepper, and salt. Bring to a gentle simmer, place lid on pot, and cook until beans are tender, anywhere from 1½ to 3 hours. Beans are funny; sometimes they cook quickly, sometimes they cook slowly. We give them the 3-bean test: Try 3 beans and check for doneness. If they are creamy and soft, you are good to go. If only 1 is soft, keep cooking.

3. Drain beans and save 3 tablespoons of liquid. Remove bay leaf.

4. Pour beans into a food processor with saved cooking liquid, lemon juice, olive oil, NOLA Smoky Andouille, and Spreadable Garlic. Purée until smooth.

5. Season to taste with salt and pepper. This dish makes a killer dip, tasty taco filling, base for a soup, and an awesome chili-style game-day burger topping.

STORAGE NOTES: *Spread will keep in the refrigerator for up to one week.*

LEAVE YOUR VEGAN GIRLFRIEND OUT OF IT *and turn the page!*

CRUNCHY
HIPSTER

Red Onion
MARMALADE PAGE 154

King **FRICO**
PAGE 77

Ballah'
PAGE 58

Raw Kale
SOFRITO PAGE 93

★ *Thick Patty*

Garlicky
RED BEAN SPREAD
PAGE 161

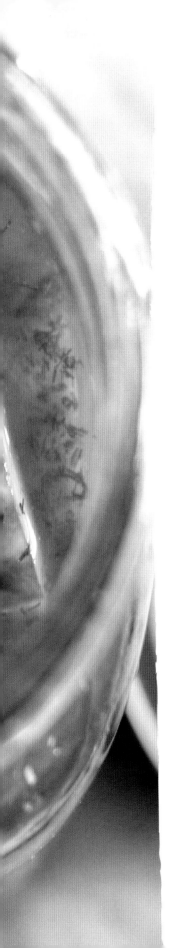

7.

WE CAN PICKLE THAT

FULL SOURS / HORSERADISH HALF SOURS / KOSHER DILL CHIPS / NEW PICKLE SANDWICH STACKERS / BREAD & BUTTER PICKLES / SPICY GARLIC PICKLES / KOOL-AID PICKLES / SWEET & SPICY BALLPARK RELISH / CHARRED CHERRY PEPPER RELISH / CHILI RELISH 57 / MUFFULETTA RELISH / CHOW-CHOW / HAMBURGER PICCALILLI / PICKLED GREEN TOMATOES / PEPPERONCINI CUBANELLES / PINEAPPLE FREEZER RELISH / PICKLED CRANBERRIES / GGS SHIITAKES

FOOD LOVERS EVERYWHERE are rediscovering and placing well-deserved value on the craft of small-batch, local, independent, American-made foodstuffs. As a result, the art of food preservation has made an epic comeback. Canning tools and jars line the shelves of hardware stores, and each summer urban homesteaders and farmers' market junkies dedicate their time to "putting up" their own stash of kickass pickled and preserved products. We can't begin to stress how integral this has been to the burger revival overall. Think about it: up until a few years ago, the only pickle anyone knew anything about was the classic cucumber dill spear or chip, which is kind of a bummer considering pickles are almost as old as mankind.

The cool, crisp, tang of a house-made pickle will balance the fatty richness of your burger and make it sing. Like every other component you can put on that badass burger you're making, the humble pickle holds a myriad of incarnations and possibilities. So turn the page and let's drop some acid.

PONDERING THE DILL PICKLE

In America, the dill pickle variety we're most familiar with is the kosher dill. And when most people picture a pickle, this is what they see. Created as early as 1899 by Jewish pickle masters of New York City, this pickle has been popularized by Jewish delis ever since. In this particular case, the term kosher does not imply that the pickle was made in accordance with Jewish dietary laws, but in line with the rules of Jewish pickle masters of the five boroughs.

This pickle—the original American dill pickle—receives its flavor and characteristics from fermentation and generous proportions of garlic, salt, and dill weed. The fermentation process entails packing cucumbers in brine, loosely covering them, and allowing them to steep at room temperature for weeks (cellar temperature, approximately 50-60°F, is ideal). When prepared with expertise, these pickles are nothing short of awesome. They may seem basic, but they set the bar for fermented pickles across the board. In fact, in his James Beard Foundation award-wining book, *The Art of Fermentation*, fermentation revivalist Sandor Katz explains that it was the brined sour cucumber pickles that sparked his interest in fermentation in the first place.

When making fermented pickles, time is the variable; the longer the cucumbers ferment, the more pungent they will become. Consequently, there are two varieties: full sours and half sours. For those interested in an extremely crisp, bright, mild pickle, half sours (and the classic fermentation method) will do the trick. For those with a more extreme palate, however, the dark green, salty, zesty full sour is the only way to go.

Maintaining a crisp texture with any pickle is a must, and when pickling via fermentation, there are many forces at play that can conspire to turn your pickles mushy. As Katz explains, "Cucumbers are extremely watery, and subject to fast decomposition by pectin-digesting enzymes. Because of these factors, it is easy to have fermented cucumbers get mushy...." The legendary food chemist Harold McGee offers a solution to this predicament. McGee recommends using unrefined sea salt in your fermenting brine, as it "improves crispiness, thanks to its calcium and magnesium impurities, which help cross-link and reinforce cell-wall pectins." Both of these cats have plenty to teach, so soak it up like a cucumber gettin' its pickle on.

Today, most of the kosher dill pickles (jarred and found on grocery shelves) are the ever-so-popular sandwich-ready dill chips, which are pickled through means of acidification. Through acidification, acid (vinegar) regulates the brine's environment and acts as the preservative. Where the fermentation process creates a funky, sour flavor profile, the acidification process yields a cleaner, snappier pickle. You can still find kosher dills made via fermentation in old school Jewish delis and specialty grocers, but it is becoming a rare breed.

When making dill pickles via acidification (vinegar pickles), be sure to use English cucumbers—we can't stress this enough. Their thin skin, firm flesh, and limited seeds create a much crunchier pickle.

....

For further reading, we recommend you pick up a copy of *The Art of Fermentation: An In-Depth Exploration of Essential Concepts and Processes from around the World* by Sandor Katz.

date: 6/17
item: Pickled Cauliflower

crafted in
sealed i

PICKLING CONTAINERS

WHEN PICKLING, it is important to always use a non-reactive container. Avoid porous containers—like wood—to prevent bacterial invasions, and avoid metallic containers—like aluminum—to prevent rust from forming. Both porous and metallic containers can cause "off" flavors.

Approved pickling containers are:

Freezer-strength resealable bags

Glass jars and plastic containers with tight-fitting lids

Porcelain and ceramic crocks

FULL SOURS

YIELD: 12 whole pickles and 12 pickled cherry peppers

START TO FINISH: 10 to 28 days   ACTIVE TIME: 1 hour

You dream of a good pickle; you're brimming with enthusiasm; you're going to ferment your own full sours. Well, welcome to the next level. We're glad you're here. However, before you get to pickling, a word to the wise: making fermented pickles is an art form that takes practice. We recommend keeping a daily journal each time you make these pickles so you can depend upon the scientific method to assist you. Don't be intimidated. Just get your geek on.

12 cups water

9 tablespoons unrefined sea salt

12 Kirby cucumbers, whole

12 cherry peppers, whole

6 grape leaves

1 huge bunch dill, whole

1 head garlic, peeled

SPECIAL EQUIPMENT:

2-gallon non-reactive
    pickling container

Fermenting stone (a ceramic
plate works, too)

Cheesecloth

Butcher's twine

1 Make brine. Boil water to sterilize. Remove from heat, add salt, and cool in the refrigerator.

2 Soak cucumbers and cherry peppers for 30 minutes in fresh, cold water. Scrub clean with a sturdy paper towel and use a butter knife to scrape off any excess root fibers and flowering buds from the ends of the cucumbers. (It's possible that there are bacteria on these ends, which will only mess with your fermentation. This extra step will bounce those bacteria straight out of the party.) Discard soaking water.

3 Pack cucumbers and cherry peppers into a 2-gallon non-reactive pickling container along with grape leaves, dill, and garlic.

4 Once brine has cooled to a temperature below 70°F, pour over container contents and place a fermenting stone or ceramic plate on top to keep pickles fully submerged. Place cheesecloth or a clean kitchen towel over the top of the container and secure with butcher's twine (this will keep pesky insects out of your tasty pickles).

5 Monitor pickles daily and skim any gunk that forms every few days. (Make sure to retie cheesecloth and butcher's twine each time.) Allow pickles to ferment for 10 to 28 days, until olive-green in color but not mushy in texture.

STORAGE NOTES: *Pickles will keep in the refrigerator for up to four weeks.*

TASTY WITH:

IPA Sesame Seed Bun,
Vermont "Velveeta,"
Magic Rings

KEEP IN MIND that under ideal conditions—a steady cellar temperature of 50-60°F, 60 percent humidity, constant darkness, and an absence of harmful microbes—a 28-day fermentation can safely occur, lending a great amount of complex flavor. However, there's a chance that long before your 28 days are up, one or more of these outside forces will find their way into your barrel and try to ruin your pickle party. That's why you must check your pickles daily, and pull them from the barrel the minute you see something afoot. We recommend checking your pickles every day after day 10 by gently squeezing them with freshly sanitized tongs or hands. Once the firm, bouncy texture begins to feel similar to a tomato going from immature to ripe, we urge you to immediately stop the fermentation process and get your goods into the refrigerator.

HORSERADISH HALF SOURS

YIELD: 12 whole pickles   START TO FINISH: 6 days   ACTIVE TIME: 1 hour

Half sours ferment in half the time that full sours do (hence the name). They're brighter, crunchier, and slightly less salty. We jacked this recipe up with fresh horseradish, marjoram, and white peppercorns; the resulting flavor profile is a cross between a Germanic and a Polish-style pickle.

12 cups water

6 tablespoons unrefined sea salt

1 tablespoon whole white peppercorn

12 Kirby cucumbers, whole

6 sprigs fresh marjoram

6 grape leaves

1 6-inch piece horseradish root, peeled and sliced into ⅛-inch thick coins

SPECIAL EQUIPMENT:

2-gallon non-reactive pickling container

Fermenting stone (a ceramic plate works, too)

Cheesecloth

Butcher's twine

1 Make brine. Boil water to sterilize. Remove from heat, add salt and peppercorns, and cool in the refrigerator.

2 Soak cucumbers and marjoram for 30 minutes in fresh, cold water. Scrub clean with a sturdy paper towel and use a butter knife to scrape off any excess root fibers and flowering buds from the ends of the cucumbers. (It's possible that there are bacteria on these ends, which will only mess with your fermentation. This extra step will bounce those bacteria straight out of the party.) Discard soaking water.

3 Pack cucumbers and marjoram into a 2-gallon non-reactive pickling container along with grape leaves and horseradish.

4 Once brine has cooled to a temperature below 70°F, pour over cucumbers and place a fermenting stone or ceramic plate on top to keep pickles fully submerged. Place cheesecloth or a clean kitchen towel over the top of the container and secure with butcher's twine (this will keep pesky insects out of your tasty pickles).

5 Monitor pickles daily and skim any gunk that forms every few days. (Make sure to retie cheesecloth and butcher's twine each time.) Allow pickles to ferment for 6 days in total.

STORAGE NOTES: *Pickles will keep in the refrigerator for up to four weeks.*

TASTY WITH:

Bacon, Scallion & Cream Cheese English Muffin, Pop's Russian, Porterhouse Tartare

KOSHER DILL CHIPS

YIELD: 2 cups   START TO FINISH: 1 day   ACTIVE TIME: 30 minutes

- 2 tablespoons dried dill weed
- 3 tablespoons kosher salt
- 3 tablespoons granulated sugar
- 1 cup distilled white vinegar
- 1 cup water
- 3 cloves garlic, peeled and smashed with back of knife
- 1 bay leaf
- 1 teaspoon crushed red pepper flakes
- 1 teaspoon whole black peppercorn
- 1 tablespoon yellow mustard seed
- 1 English cucumber, sliced into ¼-inch coins

1. Place all ingredients except for cucumbers in a pot and bring to a simmer.

2. Pack cucumbers into a 1-quart non-reactive pickling container and pour the hot pickling brine over the cucumbers.

3. Let pickles rest at room temperature for 1 hour. Seal container with tight-fitting lid and refrigerate.

4. Pickles are ready to eat after 24 hours but will be even tastier after 5 days.

STORAGE NOTES: *Dill chips will keep in the refrigerator for up to four weeks.*

TASTY WITH:

Ultimate Jewish Rye Bread, Swiss Cheese,
Polish Beet Mustard, Crispy Leeks

NEW PICKLE SANDWICH STACKERS

YIELD: 2 cups   START TO FINISH: 2 days   ACTIVE TIME: 30 minutes

Admit it, you've probably been eating the same tired, jarred, sliced pickles for as long as you've been eating sandwiches. You know you can do better. If ever a pickle were destined to grace your burger, this is probably it. Don't let your burgers have all the fun—slide these tart and herby treats into your silly little ham and cheese. It deserves this pickle, too.

1 large English cucumber

3 sprigs fresh oregano

3 sprigs fresh thyme

3 sprigs fresh rosemary

2 cups cold water

1 tablespoon unrefined sea salt

1 tablespoon granulated sugar

1 tablespoon whole
   pink peppercorn

1. Remove ends from cucumber and cut into 3 sections. Stand each section upright and slice lengthwise into ⅛-inch thick slabs.

2. Pack slices of cucumber and herbs into a 1-quart non-reactive pickling container.

3. Make brine. Pour water, salt, sugar, and pink peppercorns into a different jar that has an airtight lid.

4. Shake mixture until salt and sugar are fully dissolved, about 1 minute.

5. Pour brine into pickling container, seal, and refrigerate immediately.

6. Refrigerate for a minimum of 2 days before eating.

STORAGE NOTES: *These pickles will keep in the refrigerator for up to one week.*

TASTY WITH:

Ballah', $30 Fondue, Dijon

BREAD & BUTTER PICKLES

YIELD: 2 cups   START TO FINISH: 1 day   ACTIVE TIME: 30 minutes

We took elements of sweet pickles and bread and butter pickles and added our own spin. We mixed the high-sugar brine from the sweet with the onion and turmeric from the bread and butter and then went nuts.

We replaced mustard seed, which is standard in bread and butter pickles, with juniper berries. We love the musky, floral fragrance created by the combination of cinnamon, clove, allspice, and juniper—all classic curing ingredients. But we didn't stop there. We wanted this pickle to have a high onion content, too, and for good reason—sweet pickled onions are delicious. Be sure to pile both pickled cucumbers and onions on your burger and get the best of both worlds.

1 white onion, cut into ¼-inch thick slices

½ cup distilled white vinegar

½ cup apple cider vinegar

½ cup water

2 tablespoons kosher salt

1½ cups granulated sugar

1 cinnamon stick

7 cloves

8 juniper berries

4 allspice berries

1 teaspoon turmeric

1 large English cucumber, sliced into ¼-inch coins

1. Make brine. Place all ingredients except for cucumbers into a pot, bring to a gentle simmer, and cook for 5 minutes. Remove from heat.

2. Immediately place sliced cucumbers into pot and stir around until all ingredients are evenly incorporated.

3. Using a slotted spoon, remove cucumbers, onions, and spices and pack into a 1-quart non-reactive pickling container. Carefully pour the brine into the container, covering the ingredients inside.

4. Let pickles rest at room temperature for 1 hour. Seal container with tight-fitting lid and refrigerate.

5. Pickles are ready to eat after 24 hours but will be even tastier after 5 days.

STORAGE NOTES: Pickles will keep in the refrigerator for up to four weeks.

TASTY WITH:

Mashed Potato & Gravy Roll, Gooey Jucy Lucy, Smoked Heirlooms, Red Remoulade

SPICY GARLIC PICKLES

YIELD: 2 cups   START TO FINISH: 1 day   ACTIVE TIME: 30 minutes

These hot little numbers will give your burger a kick in the buns. Whole Fresno chiles permeate the pickling brine to give it an extra dose of spice that will make your mouth do a double take.

3 tablespoons kosher salt

2 tablespoons granulated sugar

1 cup distilled white vinegar

1 cup water

6 cloves garlic, peeled and smashed with back of knife

1 tablespoon whole green peppercorn

1 teaspoon dill seed

1 teaspoon celery seed

1 large English cucumber, sliced into ¼-inch coins

6 Fresno chiles, whole (can substitute jalapeños)

1. Make brine. Place all ingredients except for cucumbers and Fresno chiles into a pot and bring to a simmer.

2. Pack cucumbers and Fresno chiles into a 1-quart non-reactive pickling container and pour the hot pickling brine over the cucumbers and chiles.

3. Let them rest at room temperature for 1 hour. Seal container with tight-fitting lid and refrigerate.

4. Pickles are ready to eat after 24 hours but will be even tastier after 5 days.

STORAGE NOTES: *These spicy pickles will keep in the refrigerator for up to four weeks.*

TASTY WITH:

Stuffed Pretzel Bun, Vermont "Velveeta,"
Foolproof Whole Grain Mustard

KOOL-AID PICKLES

YIELD: 4 cups   START TO FINISH: 1 day   ACTIVE TIME: 15 minutes

Kool-Aid pickles are super popular throughout the Mississippi Delta. Traditionally, folks just throw store-bought whole pickles into Kool-Aid for a second wetting, almost like a remouillage of pickling. The stories we heard about kids eating bright ruby red pickles intrigued us, and we've been happy to dabble with these tart and tangy treats.

¾ cup distilled white vinegar

¾ cup water

2 tablespoons kosher salt

1½ cups granulated sugar

4 squirts of your favorite flavor of Kool-Aid Liquid (you want the concentrated drink mix)

1 English cucumber

1 Cut ends off cucumber, split in half (lengthwise), and slice ⅓-inch thick half moons. (These should be slightly thicker than a traditional pickle, because the Kool-Aid has a tendency to steal a bit of the crunch).

2 Make brine. Place all ingredients except for cucumbers into a pot and bring to a simmer.

3 Pack cucumbers into a 1-quart non-reactive pickling container and pour the hot pickling brine over the cucumbers. Let them sit at room temperature for 1 hour.

4 Seal container with a tight-fitting lid and refrigerate.

5 Pickles are ready to eat after 24 hours but will be even tastier after 5 days.

STORAGE NOTES: *Pickles will keep in the refrigerator for up to four weeks.*

TASTY WITH:

Glazed Donut with Foie-sting, Pop's Dirty Slaw, Alabama White, Chicken Fried Pork Belly

SWEET & SPICY BALLPARK RELISH

YIELD: 2 cups   START TO FINISH: 1 day   ACTIVE TIME: 30 minutes

Ballpark relish reminds us of just that: a day at the old ballpark. When Richard was growing up, his mom always pulled the kids out of school to go to opening day at Fenway Park. To this day, going to Fenway is still a magical experience: the bright green grass, the crack of the bat, and the smell of Fenway Franks lingering in the air. This relish instantly takes us back to simpler times and we think it'll do the same for you. It's damn good on a burger, but whatever your home team, we won't root against you if you dress a first-rate dog with it, too.

1 yellow onion, cut into a small dice

6 garlic cloves, minced

½ cup apple cider vinegar

½ cup distilled white vinegar

1 cup water

2 tablespoons kosher salt

2 tablespoons granulated sugar

1 tablespoon celery salt

1 tablespoon dill seed

1 tablespoon yellow mustard seed

1 tablespoon red pepper flakes

1 English cucumber, cut into a small dice

1. Place all ingredients except for cucumbers into a pot and bring to a simmer.

2. Pack cucumbers into a 1-quart non-reactive pickling container and pour the hot pickling brine over the cucumbers.

3. Let pickles rest at room temperature for 1 hour. Seal container with tight-fitting lid and refrigerate.

4. Pickles are ready to eat after 24 hours but will be even tastier after 5 days.

STORAGE NOTES: *This relish will keep in the refrigerator for up to four weeks.*

TASTY WITH:

IPA Sesame Seed Bun, Buttery Baked Robiola, Foolproof Whole Grain Mustard

CHARRED CHERRY PEPPER RELISH

YIELD: 2 cups   START TO FINISH: 3 days   ACTIVE TIME: 90 minutes

This is a simple recipe with minimal ingredients. The key to its deep flavor comes from charring the cherry peppers before the actual pickling process begins. The char adds a rich, smoky element and the caramelization gives it a pleasant sweetness. The finished product is sweet, salty, sour, and spicy, with a dash of umami.

1 pound cherry peppers, whole

2 tablespoons light olive or canola oil

3 tablespoons plus ½ teaspoon kosher salt

1½ teaspoons freshly cracked black pepper

1 cup water

1 cup apple cider vinegar

6 garlic cloves, peeled and smashed with back of knife

1 teaspoon crushed red pepper flakes

1 Preheat grill to hottest setting.

2 Toss cherry peppers in a large bowl with light olive oil or canola oil. Season gently with ½ teaspoon of salt and the black pepper.

3 Quickly char the peppers on the grill (about 3 to 4 minutes), cool slightly, and then remove stems. Place peppers into a 1-quart non-reactive pickling container.

4 Make brine. Combine water, apple cider vinegar, salt, garlic, and red pepper flakes in pot and bring to a boil.

5 Pour the hot pickling brine over the peppers. Allow the peppers to rest at room temperature for 2 hours before sealing the container with tight-fitting lid and refrigerating.

6 Let the peppers pickle for 3 days. Drain and reserve the brine, place drained cherry peppers into food processor, and coarsely chop into a relish.

7 Place chopped peppers back into quart container and pour in just enough pickling brine to cover the peppers. Save excess brine for a Bloody Mary or flaming hot pickle backs!

STORAGE NOTES: *This relish will keep in the refrigerator for up to four weeks.*

TASTY WITH:

Pizza Stromboli Bun, King Frico, Spreadable Garlic

CHILI RELISH 57

YIELD: 3 cups   START TO FINISH: 1 day   ACTIVE TIME: 15 minutes

Chili sauce was one of the original "57 varieties" offered by Heinz. Maybe. In actual fact, Henry J. Heinz just liked the way fifty-seven sounded; even back in 1892, Heinz was offering more than sixty varieties of condiments, including kooky-sounding products like plum pudding, celery soup, India relish, euchred pickles (figs), and of course, chili sauce. We took the flavor profile and commonly accepted ingredients for the Heinz Chili Sauce and whipped up this salsa-like relish.

½ English cucumber, cut into a small dice

½ pound plum tomatoes, cut into a small dice

½ green bell pepper, cut into a small dice

½ yellow onion, cut into a small dice

1 jalapeño, cut into a small dice

¼ cup white wine vinegar

2 tablespoons granulated sugar

1 tablespoon lemon juice

1 teaspoon Worcestershire (page 145 or store-bought)

¼ teaspoon cayenne

¼ teaspoon ground white peppercorn

⅛ teaspoon ground cloves

⅛ teaspoon allspice

Kosher salt and freshly cracked black pepper, to taste

1 Mix all ingredients together in a large bowl, season to taste with salt and pepper, and refrigerate overnight.

STORAGE NOTES: *Relish will keep in the refrigerator for up to one week.*

TASTY WITH:

Cincinnati Chili Bomb, Lowcountry Cornbread, Pan Fried Pickled Green Tomatoes

MUFFULETTA RELISH

YIELD: 3 cups   START TO FINISH: 1 to 5 days   ACTIVE TIME: 15 minutes

The muffuletta is a Dagwood-style Italian sandwich native to New Orleans, piled high with cured meats, several cheeses, and a quintessentially complicated olive salad. This relish is our pickled homage to that exquisite sandwich. It is a cross between a giardiniera (meaning "under vinegar," and typically eaten as an antipasto) and a tapenade.

Don't top your burger with just this relish. Go full muffuletta! Stack salami, mortadella, ham, provolone, and fresh mozzarella on your burger too. Now that we've put the idea in your head, we dare you not to try it.

½ cup mixed pitted olives, roughly chopped

½ cup cauliflower florets, roughly chopped

½ red onion, cut into a small dice

½ red bell pepper, cut into a small dice

1 celery stalk, cut into a small dice

1 medium carrot, peeled and shredded

2 tablespoons capers, roughly chopped

2 garlic cloves, minced

1 tablespoon fresh oregano, finely chopped

¼ cup red wine vinegar

¼ cup lemon juice

¼ cup extra virgin olive oil

½ teaspoon crushed red pepper flakes

Kosher salt and freshly cracked black pepper, to taste

1. Place all ingredients into a large mixing bowl.

2. Mix well and season with salt and pepper to taste.

3. Pack into a 1-quart non-reactive pickling container and refrigerate overnight.

4. This relish is ready to eat the next day but is even tastier after 5 days.

STORAGE NOTES: *Relish will keep in the refrigerator for up to two weeks.*

TASTY WITH:

NOLA Smoky Andouille, IPA Sesame Seed Bun, White Trash Chevre, Creole Mayo SEE NEXT PAGE →

Ragin' Cajun

IPA SESAME SEED **BUN**

Page 38

MUFFULETTA RELISH

Page 183

WHITE TRASH
CHEVRE

Page 83

THICK PATTY SEASONED WITH
NOLA SMOKY ANDOUILLE

Page 30

CREOLE **MAYO**

Page 135

CHOW-CHOW

YIELD: 4 cups   START TO FINISH: 1 day   ACTIVE TIME: 30 minutes

Chow-chow is quite possibly America's most diverse category of pickled relish. Ingredients vary depending on the region and can consist of green tomatoes, ripe tomatoes, chayote squash, cabbage, cauliflower, onions, carrots, and beans. Some of the most notable examples of chow-chow come from the Carolina Lowcountry, Pennsylvania Dutch area, Appalachia, Louisiana Creole and Cajun country, and the New Mexican hinterlands. This chow-chow borrows from the Lowcountry.

½ head cauliflower, roughly chopped

2 cups shredded carrots (about 8 ounces)

6 cloves garlic, thinly sliced

1 cup water

¾ cup apple cider vinegar

3 tablespoons kosher salt

2 tablespoons granulated sugar

1 bay leaf

1 teaspoon crushed red pepper flakes

2 tablespoons yellow mustard seed

1 teaspoon turmeric

1 Place cauliflower, carrots, and garlic into food processor and chop until mixture is the consistency of rice.

2 Make brine. Place water, vinegar, and all spices into a pot and bring to a simmer.

3 Pack vegetables into a non-reactive pickling container and pour the hot pickling brine over the vegetables.

4 Allow the vegetables to rest at room temperature for 1 hour before sealing the container with tight-fitting lid and refrigerating.

5 This chow-chow is ready to eat the next day but is even tastier after 3 days.

STORAGE NOTES: *Chow-chow will keep in the refrigerator for up to four weeks.*

TASTY WITH:

Beef & Rosemary Biscuit, Alabama White

HAMBURGER PICCALILLI

YIELD: 1½ cups   START TO FINISH: 1 day   ACTIVE TIME: 1 hour

Like chow-chow, piccalillis change characteristics as you travel across America. In the South, chow-chow is sometimes interchangeably called piccalilli. This particular recipe represents the classic Northeastern approach, which folks famously enjoy on hamburgers and hot dogs.

1 Vidalia onion, thinly sliced

2 tablespoons light olive oil

1 red bell pepper, thinly sliced

1 orange bell pepper, thinly sliced

½ cup granulated sugar

2 teaspoons kosher salt

2 teaspoons freshly cracked black pepper

¼ teaspoon ground allspice

½ teaspoon ground coriander

½ teaspoon granulated garlic

½ teaspoon smoked hot paprika

½ cup apple cider vinegar

1. In a large pot, over medium heat, sweat onion in olive oil until just barely translucent, about 3 minutes.

2. Add peppers and continue to sweat for 10 more minutes, stirring every minute or so, allowing them to brown slightly.

3. Add sugar, spices, and vinegar and bring to a gentle simmer. Simmer on low for 30 minutes, stirring occasionally.

4. Pack into a container and allow to fully chill in the refrigerator before covering with lid.

5. Piccalilli is ready to eat once chilled.

STORAGE NOTES: *Piccalilli will keep in the refrigerator for up to two weeks.*

TASTY WITH:

Ballah', Gooey Jucy Lucy, Mark's Ill Dip

PICKLED GREEN TOMATOES

YIELD: About 20 tomato slices   START TO FINISH: 1 day   ACTIVE TIME: 45 minutes

Pickled green tomatoes are a very common component in the cuisine of the American South. Essentially, green tomatoes are immature tomatoes. Because the growing season of tomatoes is so long in the South, growers can afford to pluck these crunchy nightshades from their vines early.

Green tomatoes are tarter than ripe red tomatoes, and they can hold up to cooking methods like pickling and frying. These treats are great as is, but if you're not afraid, take them to the next level and fry them after pickling (page 107).

6 tablespoons kosher salt

6 tablespoons granulated sugar

2 cups distilled white vinegar

2 cups water

12 cloves garlic, peeled and smashed with back of knife

1 bay leaf

2 teaspoons crushed red pepper flakes

2 teaspoons whole black peppercorn

2 tablespoons yellow mustard seed

2 cups fresh dill (about 3 ounces)

6 green tomatoes, sliced ⅓-inch thick

1 Make brine. Place all ingredients except for tomatoes and fresh dill in a pot and bring to a simmer.

2 Place dill in a 2-quart non-reactive pickling container, pack tomatoes on top, and pour the hot pickling brine over the tomatoes and dill.

3 Allow the tomatoes to rest at room temperature for 1 hour before sealing the container with tight-fitting lid and refrigerating.

4 Pickled tomatoes are ready to eat after 24 hours but will be even tastier after 5 days.

STORAGE NOTES: *These pickled green tomatoes will keep in the refrigerator for up to four weeks.*

TASTY WITH:

Southeast Peppercorn Ranch, Lowcountry Cornbread

PEPPERONCINI CUBANELLES

YIELD: 8 cups   START TO FINISH: 3 days   ACTIVE TIME: 20 minutes

These fiery pickle bombs are a cinch to pull together for a snack or your next burger extravaganza. The prep time is so quick and easy, you'll be digging into these in no time.

1½ pounds cubanelle peppers

1 habanero, split in half

¾ cup kosher salt

½ cup granulated sugar

4 cups white wine vinegar

4 cups water

1. Pierce the bottom of each cubanelle with a fork so that brine has a way to permeate the inside of the peppers.

2. Place all ingredients in a pot and gently simmer for 30 seconds.

3. Remove pot from heat and let mixture cool at room temperature for 1 hour (while still in the pot).

4. Pour everything into a 1-gallon non-reactive pickling container, seal, and refrigerate.

5. Peppers are ready to eat after 3 days but are even tastier after 7 days.

STORAGE NOTES: *These pickled cubanelles will keep in the refrigerator for four to six weeks.*

TASTY WITH:

Pizza Stromboli Bun, Semolina & Panko Crusted Burrata, Raw Kale Sofrito

PINEAPPLE FREEZER RELISH

YIELD: 6 cups   START TO FINISH: 1 day   ACTIVE TIME: 45 minutes

The freezing and thawing process "cooks" the fruits and vegetables in this relish. Here, we rely on denaturing, which occurs when the cell walls of the ingredients begin to freeze, consequently expanding to absorb the flavors of the pickling brine. In the subsequent thaw, they contract, expressing their juices and mellowing. This particular pickling process delivers a tastier relish in less time.

Since you're not applying any heat, you're not killing any naturally occurring enzymes. With these pineapples, you keep all that lovely bromelain—an enzyme loaded with health benefits, such as improving protein digestion, reducing inflammation, and treating indigestion. (And here you thought this was only a fat-ass burger book!)

1 cup rice wine vinegar

2 tablespoons kosher salt

3 tablespoons light brown sugar

1 pineapple, peeled, cored, and cut into a small dice

1 red onion, cut into a small dice

1 cup water

1 lime, zest and juice

1 tablespoon fresh ginger, peeled and grated (about a 1-inch chunk)

4 garlic cloves, minced

1. Make brine. Pour vinegar, salt, and sugar into a 1-quart non-reactive pickling container, seal, and shake until salt and sugar are fully dissolved, about 3 to 4 minutes.

2. Pour liquid into a medium bowl and toss with pineapple, red onion, water, lime zest and juice, ginger, and garlic. Place into 1-quart container and freeze, about 12 hours.

3. Defrost relish in the refrigerator before eating, approximately 12 hours. Do not refreeze once thawed.

STORAGE NOTES: *This pineapple relish will keep in the refrigerator for up to one week.*

TASTY WITH:

Astrid's Paleo Waffles, Luau Glaze, Peameal Bacon—or, for a really tasty Hawaiian treat: Spam

PICKLED CRANBERRIES

YIELD: 2 cups   START TO FINISH: 12 hours   ACTIVE TIME: 1 hour

Autumn in New England is our favorite time of year. Piles of pumpkins, leaves everywhere, and fresh cranberries that practically jump into your shopping cart, waiting to be cooked. We're all familiar with how well cranberries work with our turkey dinners, but their addition to your next charcoaled burger throwdown will blow your mind.

You can pair this with a griddled patty, but there's something enchanting about the combination of charred beef with these pickled cranberries. So make sure you get one last session in before stashing your grill away for the winter months.

2 cups fresh cranberries (frozen cranberries work in a pinch, but nothing beats the fresh stuff)

3 sprigs fresh thyme

3 sprigs fresh rosemary

1 cup granulated sugar

3 tablespoons kosher salt

1 cup apple cider vinegar

1 cup water

3 whole cloves

3 whole allspice berries

2 cinnamon sticks

1 Combine all ingredients in a large pot, bring to a gentle simmer, and cook until the cranberries just begin to burst, about 5 to 8 minutes. Immediately remove from heat and let sit at room temperature for 1 hour.

2 Pour the contents into a 1-quart non-reactive pickling container, seal, and refrigerate overnight.

3 Cranberries are ready to eat after 12 hours but are even tastier after 3 days.

STORAGE NOTES: *Pickled cranberries will keep in the refrigerator for up to four weeks.*

TASTY WITH:

Mashed Potato & Gravy Roll, Vidalia Jam, Coconut Sweet Potato Tots

GGS SHIITAKES
Adapted from David Chang's Momofuku

YIELD: 4 cups   START TO FINISH: 1 day   ACTIVE TIME: 45 minutes

Even if you aren't a huge lover of the fungi, we think you'll enjoy these snappy little bastards. Soy sauce and mushrooms are practically BFFs, and this umami-packed pickle will soon become one of your favorite burger toppings.

We've adapted our recipe from *Momofuku* by David Chang. Entirely unknown to one another and on separate occasions, we each followed his pickled shiitake recipe and we were like, "Man, that's an insanely good pickle."

Chang's use of ginger in his recipe inspired us to add more aromatics and complete the GGS flavor profile (ginger, garlic, and scallion). Chinese cooking relies heavily on this trio for good reason; it's a great way to add a clean brightness and rich depth to any dish.

4 cups dried, whole shiitakes

1 bunch scallions, thinly sliced

½ cup granulated sugar

1 cup soy sauce

1 cup balsamic vinegar

½ cup mirin

3-inch hunk fresh ginger, peeled and smashed with back of a knife

4 cloves garlic, peeled and smashed with back of a knife

1 Rehydrate mushrooms. Place in pot, cover with water, bring to a simmer, place lid on pot, and remove from heat. Steep for 15 minutes, drain mushrooms, and reserve 2 cups of steeping water for brine.

2 Strain 2 cups of reserved steeping liquid through a fine mesh sieve to remove any dirt.

3 Remove stems of mushrooms, discard, and slice caps into ¼-inch thick slices. Place in a 2-quart non-reactive pickling container with sliced scallions.

4 Make brine. Combine sugar, soy sauce, vinegar, mirin, ginger, garlic, and reserved steeping liquid in a pot and bring to a simmer.

5 Immediately pour over mushrooms and scallions. Let them sit at room temperature for 1 hour, seal, and refrigerate.

6 Shiitakes are ready to eat after 24 hours but are even tastier after 5 days.

STORAGE NOTES: *These shiitakes will keep in the refrigerator for up to four weeks.*

TASTY WITH:

Ballah', Watercress, Chive & Cream Cheese Spread, Steak Sauce, Porterhouse Tartare, Magic Rings

....

Anyone thinking...steakhouse? SEE NEXT PAGE →

THE

Delmonico

BALLAH'
Page 58

THICK
PATTY

8.

JUNK DRAWER

PORTERHOUSE TARTARE / 11-HOUR CORNED BEEF HASH / JAMMY YOLKS / JOHNNYCAKE FRIED OYSTERS / CHICKEN FRIED PORK BELLY / SMOKED TASSO HAM / PEAMEAL BACON / SPREADABLE GARLIC / EXTRA SPICY BLACK GARLIC KIMCHI / COCONUT SWEET POTATO TOTS / MAGIC RINGS / HOP HEAD CURLY FRIES / CHEESEBURGER MANHATTAN / STRAWBERRY SRIRACHA PUSH POPS / "MEZCAL MULE" COMPRESSED WATERMELON / OLD FASHIONED SARSAPARILLA

AS A CHILD, the junk drawer was the shit. Pure magic. Opening it up, sifting through all its layers of trash and treasure, hoping to find the missing arm to your Donatello action figure, trying not to get stabbed by that *one* sharp object. You never knew what the junk drawer would bring.

Well, that's exactly what this chapter is—a hodgepodge of random burger-related schwag that doesn't really belong in the other chapters. Put these offerings on top of your burger or on the side; eat them with your burger or eat them after; let some of them get you drunk. Keep these recipes in mind as you plan your next burger feast. The recipes in this chapter flaunt some of our favorite flavors and utilize a range of cooking techniques, from classic French to the hijinks of the contemporary kitchen—all with the one goal of adding that little something extra every righteous burger needs.

PORTERHOUSE TARTARE

YIELD: 1¼ cups   START TO FINISH: 10 minutes

This tartare gives you the best of both worlds. You get the mild melt-in-your-mouth texture of the beef tenderloin and the meaty, well-marbled chew of the New York strip steak. Be sure to trim off excess exterior fat, gristle, and silver skin.

1 16-ounce cut of beef porterhouse, deboned

½ teaspoon Worcestershire (page 145 or store-bought)

2 teaspoons freshly squeezed lemon juice

2 teaspoons minced garlic

1 tablespoon minced shallot

1 tablespoon fresh parsley, roughly chopped

2 tablespoons Foolproof Whole Grain Mustard (page 127 or store-bought)

1 egg yolk

Kosher salt and freshly cracked black pepper, to taste

1. Keep beef ice cold until handling. Using a sharp knife, finely mince beef. To do so, slice beef into thin strips, then repeat the process so that those slices are even thinner. Continue by dicing into small cubes. Mince until you've achieved a fine texture that clumps together. Place beef in a chilled stainless steel bowl, and place bowl over an ice bath.

2. Place remaining ingredients in the bowl with the beef and mix together until uniform. Season to taste with salt and pepper.

3. Spread on your burger or plate up as a meat-on-meat side dish with grilled bread, mustard, and your favorite pickles. Serve immediately for freshest flavor.

STORAGE NOTES: *Store in a resealable bag in the refrigerator. Make sure to squeeze all the air out to avoid oxidation and that undesirable browning color. Eat within twenty-four hours.*

TASTY WITH:

Toasted Baguette, Foolproof Whole Grain Mustard, Spicy Garlic Pickles

11-HOUR CORNED BEEF HASH

YIELD: 8 to 10 cups   START TO FINISH: 11 hours   ACTIVE TIME: 1 hour

The key to making great hash is time and patience—especially when you sous vide your brisket. That said, it's easy as pie to toss your meat into the bath and hit the hay. The true test comes when you turn this magnificent meat into hash, allowing your corned beef, spices, potatoes, and onions to caramelize and crisp in five-minute intervals without interruption. When you stir the hash and scrape the pan, be sure to get all the crunchy little num nums that have formed on the bottom. Otherwise, you deserve to get that pan right upside your head, Baby Sinclair style. Those speckles of brown are "the mama" when it comes to flavor. (The French call it *fond*.) It will add depth, texture, and succulence to your hash. If you don't scrape, eventually it will cake and burn. Heed our advice and your patience will be rewarded with the best hash you've ever had.

1 fresh (brined and uncooked) corned beef brisket, about 3 pounds

2 tablespoons coriander seed, finely ground

1 tablespoon fennel seed, finely ground

1 tablespoon mustard seed, finely ground

1½ tablespoons whole black peppercorn, finely ground

1½ pounds Russet potatoes

2 medium yellow onions

2 tablespoons olive oil

¼ pound good unsalted butter

Kosher salt and freshly cracked black pepper, to taste

SPECIAL EQUIPMENT:

Sous vide machine

Vacuum food sealer

1. Place sous vide machine in water bath and set temperature to 180°F.

2. Remove corned beef brisket from its packaging, rinse thoroughly under cold water, and pat dry with paper towels.

3. Rub corned beef with coriander, fennel seed, mustard seed, and ground black peppercorns. Place in food saver bag and vacuum seal.

4. Once the water reaches a temperature of 180°F, place vacuum-sealed brisket in water bath and cook for 10 hours.

5. In the meantime, peel and cut potatoes and onions into a small dice. Place in a large bowl and lightly toss with olive oil. Season with salt and freshly cracked black pepper.

6. Pack potatoes and onions in a food saver bag and vacuum seal.

7. At the 8½-hour mark, add the bag of potatoes and onions to the water bath. At 10 hours, remove everything.

8. Open both bags and drain excess liquid. Allow corned beef to cool enough to handle and cut into a small dice.

CHANCES ARE you may not find brined and uncooked corned beef unless it's St. Patty's day. That's sad. But here's the good news: Make this recipe and you won't have to wait for March 17th to enjoy the best hash of your life. For the sake of convenience, prepare the recipe as directed and simply portion and freeze what you don't eat. Take it out and have yourself a killer breakfast whenever you want. Sláinte, yo.

9   In a very large cast iron skillet or carbon steel wok, melt butter over medium heat.

10   Add meat, potatoes, and onions to skillet or wok.

11   Allow hash to cook in 5-minute intervals without interruption. Then stir, scrape, and repeat, cooking for a total of 45 minutes. Season to taste with salt and pepper.

12   Pile hash on top of your burger for the ultimate breakfast experience any time of day.

STORAGE NOTES: *Hash will keep in the refrigerator for up to five days or in the freezer for up to three months.*

TASTY WITH:

Beef & Rosemary Biscuit, Red Rooster, Jammy Yolks

ADDING A FRIED EGG to your burgers is as old school as the sidecar diner, but over the past decade, this sunny side up accoutrement has become a mainstream phenomenon. And for good reason. The experience of eating a burger topped with a fried egg is pure bliss, from the first bite's eggy pop, to the last bite's plate sopping swoosh, and every congealed-yolk-on-chin moment in between.

From sunny side up to over easy, classically poached to the more modern slow cooked, or just simply fried, we think there's almost always a good reason to put an egg on your next burger. And don't stop there; get funky with with. Why not try adding a cheese omelette, frittata, or tortilla espanola to your next massive masterpiece? You can add a unique layer to your burger with a simple crack of an egg.

JAMMY YOLKS

YIELD: 4 eggs   START TO FINISH: 100 minutes   ACTIVE TIME: 10 minutes

If you're a fan of adding a fried egg to your burger and you dig trying new techniques, this is the recipe for you. You'll get all of that yolky goodness in a spreadable, portable ball. Call it nature's little condiment packet.

Essentially, you're using your sous vide machine to make what professional chefs refer to as slow cooked eggs. It may sound exotic, but there's very little to it. Chefs love them because they're impossible to screw up. You simply set the temperature of your bath to yield a desired doneness of yolk (and white) and ninety minutes later, your eggs are done. Perfectly. Every time. And it gets better. You can cook one or one hundred eggs this way. They'll take the same amount of time, and they'll all be perfect. (This recipe calls for four eggs, but honestly, you can cook as many eggs as you can fit and eat at any given time. So keep this in mind when throwing big backyard barbecues and Sunday brunches.)

4 good chicken eggs (the best you can get)

Kosher salt and freshly cracked black pepper, to taste

SPECIAL EQUIPMENT:

Sous vide machine

1. Submerge sous vide machine into a water bath and set the temperature 147°F.

2. Once the water reaches that temperature, gently place eggs in bath for 90 minutes.

3. Remove eggs from bath, carefully crack them open, and extract the yolks. Gently discard the whites and rinse the yolks in the water bath to wash off any remaining egg whites.

4. Schmear yolk on burger or bun, and season with salt and pepper.

STORAGE NOTES: *Yolks must be used right away.*

TASTY WITH:

Portlandia Dry Rub, Bacon, Scallion & Cream Cheese English Muffin, Fried Ketchup

JOHNNYCAKE FRIED OYSTERS

YIELD: 12 to 15 oysters   START TO FINISH: 20 minutes

Thanks to the good state of Rhode Island, we have Johnnycakes, a traditional cornmeal pancake. When we want to go all New England, we use this Johnnycake batter with a hit of bacon to deep fry oysters. They make an amazing topping for a surf and turf burger. What cheer!

4 cups oil, for frying

2 strips bacon, cooked and minced, all fat reserved

½ cup corn flour

¼ cup all-purpose flour

½ cup whole milk

1 egg

½ teaspoon kosher salt

¼ teaspoon cayenne

8 ounces shucked oysters (about 12 to 15 oysters)

Old Bay seasoning, to taste

1. Heat the frying oil to 375°F (see Frying Guide on page xiv).

2. In a medium bowl, whisk together bacon, bacon fat, and both flours with milk, egg, salt, and cayenne.

3. Dip each oyster into batter and place directly into hot oil.

4. Fry for 3 minutes, remove from oil, place on brown paper bag, and season immediately with Old Bay. Lots and lots of Old Bay.

5. Top each burger with 2 or 3 fried oysters while everything is still hot.

STORAGE NOTES: *Fried foods don't keep, so eat these suckers up.*

TASTY WITH:

IPA Sesame Seed Bun, Pop's Russian, Peameal Bacon

CHICKEN FRIED PORK BELLY

YIELD: 18 to 24 pieces   START TO FINISH: 2 days   ACTIVE TIME: 2 hours

It doesn't get more luxurious and decadent than this. We treat the pork belly with love: rubbing it with cure, bathing it for hours in a sous vide hot tub, soaking it in a buttermilk marinade, dredging it with the finest seasonings, and finally frying it to a crisp, golden brown, meaty masterpiece. It's insane on its own, on a burger, or eaten "Lady and the Tramp" style with that special someone.

3 pounds pork belly, skin off

6 tablespoons kosher salt, plus more to taste

3 tablespoons granulated sugar

1 cup buttermilk

2 eggs

Freshly cracked black pepper, to taste

1 cup self-rising flour

1 teaspoon poultry seasoning

1 teaspoon cayenne

4 cups light olive oil or canola oil, for frying

SPECIAL EQUIPMENT:

Sous vide machine

Vacuum food sealer

1 Cure belly. Remove skin if purchased with skin on. Mix 6 tablespoons of salt and 3 tablespoons of sugar together and season all sides of belly. Vacuum seal the belly and refrigerate for 24 hours.

2 Sous vide pork. Remove belly from refrigerator, rinse under cold water until all cure is washed away, and pat dry with paper towels. Place belly in food saver bag and vacuum seal. Submerge sous vide machine into a water bath and set the temperature to 170°F. Once bath has reached the set temperature, place vacuum-sealed belly in water and circulate for 18 hours.

3 Handling carefully (your belly is now extremely tender and delicate), remove pork from bag, discard any rendered liquid fat and juices, and lay on sheet pan lined with parchment. Refrigerate until fully chilled, at least 4 hours. Using a very sharp knife (so you don't mangle your pork), slice belly into 1/3-inch thick slabs, and then cut each slab in half, yielding 3- to 4-inch long pieces, depending on the original width of your belly.

4 Marinate belly. Whisk buttermilk and eggs together, season with a pinch of salt and pepper, add pork, and refrigerate for 6 to 12 hours.

5 Coat and fry belly. Heat your frying oil to 350°F (see Frying Guide on page xiv). In a medium bowl, mix flour with poultry spice and cayenne. Remove pork from marinade, shake off excess liquid, drop into dredge,

and evenly coat all sides of belly. Drop dredged belly into fryer and cook pieces in batches until golden brown and crispy on the outside and hot and succulent on the inside, about 3 minutes.

6 Immediately place onto a brown paper bag and lightly season with salt and pepper.

STORAGE NOTES: *Eat this pork belly straight out of the fryer. The sous vide belly will keep in marinade in the refrigerator for up to four days.*

TASTY WITH:

Southeast Peppercorn Ranch, Lowcountry Cornbread, Quick Pickled Red Onions, Bourbon Barrel Red Hot

SMOKED TASSO HAM

YIELD: 3 pounds of ham   START TO FINISH: 1 week   ACTIVE TIME: 2 hours

We love stacking thinly shaved Tasso ham on our burgers. Toss it in a skillet, melt out some of the fat, and crisp it up quickly. It's good enough to debut as the star of your next sandwich but tastes out-of-this-world on a burger. The recipe yields plenty of Tasso ham, so go wild! Cut it into a small dice and render it with aromatics when preparing soups and stews, use in place of pancetta to make one hell of a good Americana carbonara, or shave it and hook yourself up with a spicy Croque Monsieur. Just be sure to save some for your next batch of burgers.

3 pounds boneless pork butt

2 quarts water

½ cup kosher salt

2 tablespoons granulated sugar

1 teaspoons Insta Cure™ No. 1

TASSO SPICE RUB

2 tablespoons freshly cracked black pepper

2 tablespoons brown sugar

2 tablespoons kosher salt

2 tablespoons smoked paprika

1 tablespoon ground chipotle

1 tablespoon cayenne

SPECIAL EQUIPMENT:

20-pound capacity smoker

1. Cut pork butt into 1-inch thick slabs, making sure meat is clean of all gristle and sinew. Slabs should be about 3 inches to 5 inches wide.

2. In a small pot, bring 2 cups of water to a simmer. Remove from heat and add salt, sugar, and Insta Cure™. Stir until dissolved.

3. Place meat into a large container with 6 cups of cold water and pour salt solution into the mix. Mix to quickly cool the hot liquid.

4. Brine for 7 days in refrigerator.

5. After 7 days, remove pork from brine, rinse thoroughly under cold water, and pat dry.

6. Set your smoker to 225°F and begin generating smoke.

7. In a medium bowl, mix ingredients together for Tasso spice rub. Thoroughly dredge each piece of meat with seasoning. You want a nice, even, thin layer. Go easy; too much spice will result in a cakey exterior.

8. Evenly distribute the brined, seasoned ham throughout your smoker and cook for 90 minutes.

9. Rest meat for 15 minutes before slicing into thin strips.

STORAGE NOTES: *Tasso ham will keep in the refrigerator for up to one week. You can also vacuum seal and freeze it for up to three months.*

INSTA CURE™ NO. 1 is a preservative salt used in cures and brines for to-be-cooked meats, which boosts shelf life and blesses your meat with that aesthetically pleasing pink finish. (Who wants to eat grey ham?) This particular blend contains salt and sodium nitrite (6.25 percent) and is readily available online or from your favorite specialty kitchen store.

PEAMEAL BACON

YIELD: 20 slices of bacon   START TO FINISH: 1 week   ACTIVE TIME: 1 hour

It's not quite Canadian bacon (or "Back Bacon" as Hope and Mark Chudy call it), but it's just as delicious. At the St. Lawrence market in Toronto, Carousel Bakery sells the best Peameal Bacon sandwiches. Instead of being smoked, the bacon is cooked on a griddle and coated with cornmeal. These thin slices of pork loin are a dream with mustard, but they're even better crisped up and topped on a fat burger.

(Richard couldn't be more Canadian if he tried, eh?)

3 quarts water

1 cup maple syrup (preferably with a Mountie or maple leaf on the bottle)

⅔ cup kosher salt

1 teaspoon Insta Cure™ No. 1

2 tablespoons whole black peppercorn

6 whole cloves

¼ cup fresh sage

½ cup mustard of your choice

2 bay leaves

3 pounds boneless pork loin, excess fat trimmed

4 to 5 tablespoons cornmeal, for dusting

2 to 3 tablespoons light olive oil or canola oil

1. In a pot large enough to hold the pork loin, bring the water, maple syrup, salt, Insta Cure™, peppercorns, cloves, sage, mustard, and bay leaves to a boil. Cool to room temperature, and then place in the refrigerator until the internal temperature is 40°F (an overnight stay should do the trick).

2. Add the pork loin to the cooled brine. Keeping the pork submerged with a plate if necessary, cover and refrigerate for 5 days.

3. After 5 days, remove the pork loin from the fridge and rinse under cold water. Dry well with paper towels.

4. Roll the pork in enough cornmeal to cover the outside completely and place on a rack on a baking sheet. Refrigerate for 12 to 24 hours.

5. Slice the pork into ¼-inch thick slices.

6. Heat a large griddle or skillet over medium-high heat and add enough oil to lightly coat the pan. Add the pork in batches. Cook until the pork is cooked through in the center and the edges are crispy, about 2 to 3 minutes per side. Repeat as needed.

7. Stack this bacon on top of your next burger. Slather any leftovers in mustard for a crispy, salty meat snack, stuff into your breakfast omelettes, or inhale straight out of the fridge during commercial breaks.

STORAGE NOTES: *Peameal bacon will keep uncooked in the refrigerator for up to one week or in the freezer for up to three months. Before freezing, be sure to slice it and bag it into desired potions for convenience.*

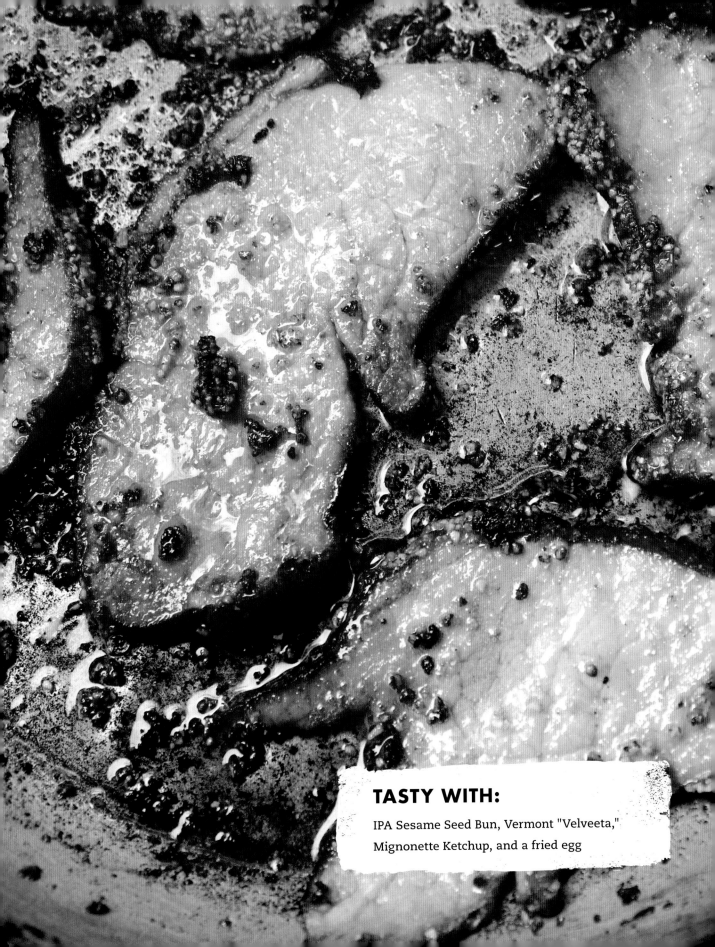

TASTY WITH:

IPA Sesame Seed Bun, Vermont "Velveeta,"
Mignonette Ketchup, and a fried egg

SPREADABLE GARLIC

YIELD: 2 cups   START TO FINISH: 2 hours   ACTIVE TIME: 5 minutes

Roasting garlic releases a mellow sweetness that complements almost anything. Spread this baby every which way you like; on burgers, sandwiches, pizza, grilled cheese sandwiches, the sky's the limit. We think you'll find plenty of excuses to use it.

1 cup peeled garlic cloves (about 2 to 3 heads)

1 cup light olive oil

Pinch kosher salt

1. Preheat oven to 250°F.

2. Remove fibrous root ends of the garlic cloves.

3. Place garlic and olive oil into an oven-safe dish that is small enough to ensure that all the garlic is fully submerged in oil.

4. Triple-wrap the top of the dish with plastic wrap. (Don't worry! The plastic wrap won't melt at this temperature.) Cover wrapped dish with aluminum foil.

5. Bake for 90 minutes.

6. Remove from oven and let cool for 30 minutes before uncovering.

7. Transfer roasted garlic and oil into a small bowl and gently mash with a fork.

8. Spread on everything. Lick knife clean.

STORAGE NOTES: *Spread will keep in the refrigerator for up to two weeks.*

TASTY WITH:

Cincinnati Chili Bomb, Beef & Rosemary Biscuit, Bread & Butter Pickles

EXTRA SPICY BLACK GARLIC KIMCHI

YIELD: 2 cups   START TO FINISH: 1 week   ACTIVE TIME: 1 hour

Black garlic is sweet and savory with rich, tangy notes of balsamic, molasses, and tamarind. Contrary to popular belief, black garlic is not fermented but rather slowly cooked at an extremely low temperature for several weeks. The end result is sticky, resinous cloves packed with a dank flavor and nearly twice the amount of antioxidants as raw garlic. If you can't find black garlic (or don't wish to cough up the extra scratch to score some), simply substitute with four cloves of minced, fresh garlic.

3 tablespoons kosher salt

3 tablespoons granulated sugar

1 head Napa cabbage, washed, dried, cored, and cut into 1-inch by 1-inch squares

1 bunch scallions, cut into 1-inch pieces

4 cloves black garlic, peeled and minced

1-inch ginger root, peeled and minced

1 teaspoon crushed red pepper flakes

2 tablespoons Red Rooster (page 148 or sriracha)

1 tablespoon fish sauce

1 Cure cabbage. Mix salt and sugar together. Place cut cabbage into a large mixing bowl. Lightly coat cabbage with salt and sugar. Place cabbage into a 1-gallon resealable freezer bag and rest at room temperature for 12 hours.

2 Start kimchi. Remove cured cabbage, gently squeeze out excess liquid, and place in a large mixing bowl. Discard any liquid left over from the curing process. Add scallions, black garlic, ginger, pepper flakes, Red Rooster, and fish sauce to bowl. Mix until all ingredients are evenly incorporated.

3 Ferment kimchi. Place mixture into a plastic or glass container, wrap entire container liberally with plastic wrap, poke 10 tiny air holes in the top of plastic (we use a cake tester), and allow kimchi to ferment at room temperature for 3 days before placing in refrigerator.

4 Kimchi is ready after 3 full days of fermentation but will continue to develop flavors while refrigerated. In our opinion, it tastes best when given an additional 3 weeks in your refrigerator.

STORAGE NOTES: *Kimchi will keep in the refrigerator for up to three months.*

TASTY WITH:

Ballah', Charred Marinated Scallions, Miso Curry Mayo

Feeling fired up? Add cilantro and a fried egg. SEE NEXT PAGE →

MISO HORNY

CHARRED MARINATED
SCALLIONS
Page 109

FRIED
EGG

EXTRA SPICY
BLACK GARLIC KIMCHI
Page 219

BALLAH'
Page 58

CILANTRO

THICK PATTY

MISO
CURRY MAYO
Page 134

COCONUT SWEET POTATO TOTS

YIELD: 4 servings   START TO FINISH: 1 hour   ACTIVE TIME: 30 minutes

We loved tots as kids, and we're not ashamed to admit that we love them as adults, too. This recipe deviates from those lunchroom spuds of yore by incorporating the lush flavors of sweet potatoes and coconut.

2 pounds sweet potatoes, peeled and shredded

¼ cup light olive oil or canola oil, plus 4 cups for frying

¼ cup coconut flakes

2 teaspoons kosher salt, plus more to taste

1 cup cornstarch, divided

Freshly cracked black pepper, to taste

1 In a large pot over medium heat, sweat sweet potatoes in ¼ cup oil until tender but still slightly crunchy, about 5 to 7 minutes.

2 Remove from oil and spread potatoes on sheet tray. Refrigerate for 30 minutes.

3 After potatoes have been in refrigerator for 25 minutes, heat the frying oil to 350°F (see Frying Guide on page xiv).

4 In a large bowl, mix cooled sweet potatoes with coconut flakes, salt, and ¼ cup cornstarch.

5 Using your hands, form sweet potato mixture into small logs, approximately 1½-inches long and ¾-inch thick; make sure the logs are well formed and tightly packed.

6 Put ¾ cup of cornstarch into a medium bowl. Dredge each tot. (After 5 tots are dredged, start frying.)

7 Deep fry tots until golden brown, about 3 to 4 minutes. With a slotted spoon, remove tots from oil and place onto a brown paper bag.

8 Season immediately with salt and pepper.

STORAGE NOTES: *You won't have to worry about storing leftovers because there won't be any. You can, however, prepare this mixture one day in advance and keep it in the refrigerator. Just don't dredge the tots in the cornstarch until it's frying time.*

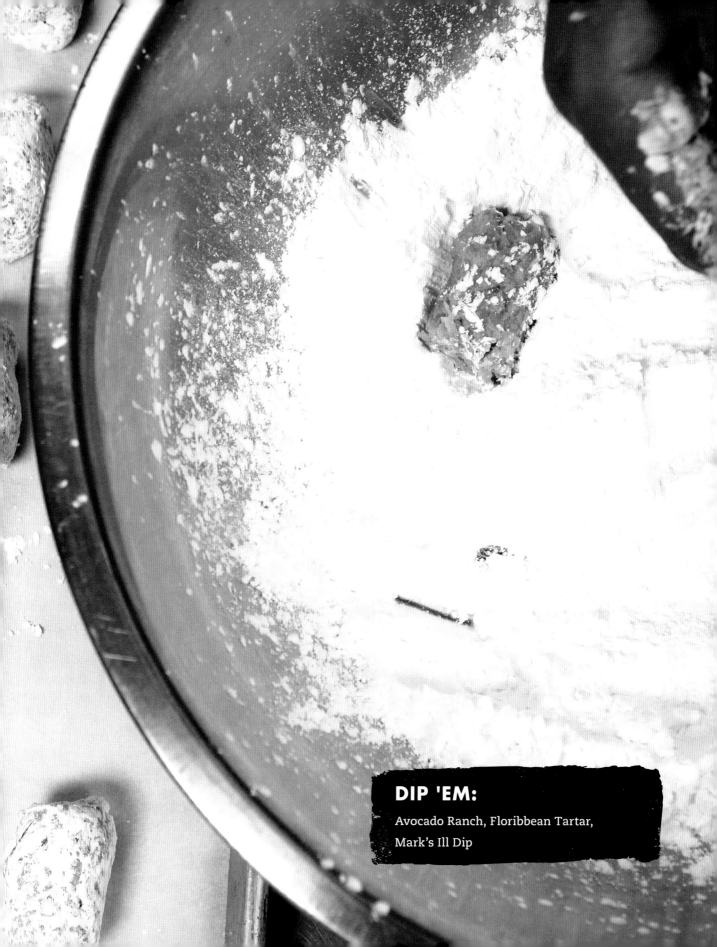

DIP 'EM:

Avocado Ranch, Floribbean Tartar, Mark's Ill Dip

MAGIC RINGS

YIELD: 4 servings   START TO FINISH: About 30 to 45 minutes

Onion rings are finicky, no question about it. Too often, the entire onion either comes out of its fried batter shell in one bite, or the onion is cut so thin that the ring ends up being all batter.

The real secret to creating the perfect onion ring lies in the frying temperature. We fry these babies at 400°F to break down the onion, ensuring it isn't raw and crunchy. We use vodka in our batter because its high-alcohol percentage aids in the reduction of gluten formation, yielding a tender yet crisp melt-in-your-mouth exterior. The alcohol rapidly evaporates once it hits the fryer oil, and since vodka is a neutral spirit, these magic rings will have no boozy aftertaste. (In other words, feel free to use bottom-shelf Aristocrat.)

There are a million ways to flavor and spice these guys; pick out your favorite dry rub from *Spice the Nation* (page 21), and upon removing your rings from the fryer, generously dust with your seasoning of choice.

1 cup all-purpose flour

1 tablespoon kosher
   salt, plus more
   to taste

1 cup cornstarch

1 tablespoon baking
   powder

1 cup water

1 cup vodka

4 cups canola or peanut
   oil, for frying

4 large Vidalia onions,
   cut into ½-inch
   thick rings

1. In a large bowl, whisk the flour, 1 tablespoon salt, cornstarch, and baking powder together.

2. In a separate bowl, stir the water and vodka together. Slowly pour the liquid mixture into the flour mixture and gently stir to combine. It should be like thick pancake batter, so add more water to thin as needed.

3. Heat the frying oil to 400°F (see Frying Guide on page xiv). Add the onion rings to the batter and stir to coat. When oil reaches 400°F, carefully place rings in oil and fry until golden brown. Cook in batches, about 3 to 5 minutes per batch.

4. With a slotted spoon, remove rings from oil and place onto a brown paper bag. Sprinkle with salt (or dry seasoning of your choice) while they are still warm.

5. Repeat until all the rings are fried, making sure the oil returns to 400°F in between batches.

6. Smash in mouth, top on burger, or give to your favorite neighbor Christmas morning.

STORAGE NOTES: *These rings won't store well, so eat 'em up.*

TASTY WITH:

IPA Sesame Seed Bun, KFC Buffalo Blue Cheese, Grilled Romaine Hearts, Smoked Heirlooms

HOP HEAD CURLY FRIES

YIELD: 2 to 4 servings   START TO FINISH: 1¼ hours   ACTIVE TIME: 15 minutes

Traditionally, good fries are cooked twice; first they are blanched in oil at a low temperature (325°F) to cook the potato without developing any browning, then they are cooked a second time at a higher temperature (375°F) to develop that distinct golden brown crispiness. Soaking cut potatoes in IPA means no blanching. With this recipe, you get kickass flavor and save a step. Boom.

Up the ante with the Citra Hop Seasoning and Cascade Malt Vinegar—a powerful combination that is utterly addictive. Citra hops have a musky, citrus aroma, while Cascade hops boast a fragrant, flowery bouquet. Both are available in health food stores, through home brew suppliers, or online.

CITRA HOP SEASONING

2 tablespoons kosher salt

1 tablespoon granulated sugar

1 teaspoon Citra pellet hops, crushed with fingers into powder

Zest of ½ lemon

CASCADE MALT VINEGAR

1 cup malt vinegar

2 teaspoons Cascade pellet hops, crushed with fingers into powder

CURLY FRIES

2 large Russet potatoes, scrubbed clean

24 ounces IPA

1 tablespoon kosher salt

4 cups canola oil or peanut oil, for frying

SPECIAL EQUIPMENT:

Spiral vegetable cutter

1 Make Citra hop seasoning. Mix seasoning ingredients together in a small bowl and set aside until ready to season fries.

2 Make malt vinegar. Pour vinegar into squeeze bottle, add hops, and let steep at room temperature for 1 hour. Refrigerate until ready to use. (This malt vinegar will keep in the refrigerator for up to 6 months.)

3 Prepare the potatoes. Run the potatoes through the spiral cutter. As the fries are cut, immediately soak them in IPA seasoned with salt. Soak for at least 1 hour and no more than 4 hours. Drain thoroughly.

4 Heat the frying oil to 375°F (see Frying Guide on page xiv) and begin frying the potatoes in batches until golden brown and crispy, about 3 to 4 minutes per batch.

5 With a slotted spoon, remove fries from oil and place onto a brown paper bag. Sprinkle with Citra seasoning. Repeat steps 2 and 3 until all fries are cooked.

6 Enjoy with Cascade Malt Vinegar and any other funky dunking condiments you've got on hand.

STORAGE NOTES: *Fried foods don't keep, so eat these babies right away.*

TASTY WITH:

Stuffed Pretzel Bun, Pimento EZ CHZ, Umami Ketchup, "Burn Your Nose Hairs" Yellow Mustard, Sweet & Spicy Ballpark Relish

LOOKING FOR A GAME CHANGER?
LAY SOME DOGS ON THAT BURGER, TOO!

Turn the page to see this combo in action! →

STUFFED PRETZEL BUN
Page 52

SWEET & SPICY BALLPARK RELISH
Page 179

SPLIT GRILLED HOT DOGS

THE NEW *American* PASTIME

HOP HEAD
CURLY FRIES
Page 226

PIMENTO EZ CHZ
Page 73

"BURN YOUR NOSE HAIRS"
YELLOW MUSTARD
Page 128

UMAMI KETCHUP
Page 119

SWEET DILL PICKLED CIPOLLINI ONIONS

YIELD: Garnish for 8 to 10 drinks

1 cup distilled white vinegar

1 cup water

3 tablespoons granulated sugar

3 tablespoons kosher salt

1 tablespoon whole green peppercorn

1 teaspoon dill seed

½ teaspoon crushed red pepper flakes

½ teaspoon dried Mexican oregano

½ teaspoon dried marjoram

1 bay leaf

2 cloves garlic, peeled and smashed with back of knife

12 Cipollini onions, ends removed and peeled

2 tablespoons fresh dill

1. Place all ingredients except for onions and fresh dill in a pot and simmer for 1 minute.

2. Place fresh dill in the bottom of a 1-quart non-reactive fermenting container with a sealable lid (see page 167 for more information on pickling containers), pack onions on top, and pour pickling brine over top.

3. Allow onions to rest at room temperature for 1 hour. Seal container with tight-fitting lid and refrigerate at least 1 day before using as a garnish for the cocktail.

STORAGE NOTES: *These pickled onions will keep in the refrigerator for up to three weeks.*

SMOKED SUET WASHED BOOKER'S BOURBON

YIELD: 16 to 20 ounces of fat-washed whiskey, or enough for 8 to 10 cocktails

750 ml Booker's bourbon

1 pound beef suet, diced into 1-inch chunks

SPECIAL EQUIPMENT:

Cold smoker • Hickory chips • Cheesecloth

✱ *Make sure your smoker can cold smoke. The fat must remain uncooked so it does not render, which is why it smokes at 85°F.*

1. Cold smoke beef suet at 85°F with hickory chips for 2 hours.

2. In a medium saucepot over low heat, render suet for 1 hour. Keep lid on pot so suet can "steam," and stir every 10 minutes to ensure even rendering.

3. Remove beef fat from heat and allow to rest in pot for 10 minutes. Do not handle fat while it rests.

4. Strain suet through a fine mesh sieve and pour into a 2-quart non-reactive container. Pour bourbon into same container.

5. Stir rigorously with a spoon for 90 seconds.

6. Allow bourbon and fat to sit at room temperature for 6 hours, then chill in freezer overnight.

7. Moving quickly to keep it cold, strain bourbon into a clean container through a fine mesh sieve lined with cheesecloth.

STORAGE NOTES: *Because there is animal product in the whiskey, we prefer to play it safe and store this in the freezer. Whiskey will keep for up to three months.*

CHEESEBURGER MANHATTAN

YIELD: 1 cocktail

This cocktail was the result of some serious mad science and a lot of education from our homie Seth Freidus, a Boston-area mixologist. And because of Seth's help, this cocktail is a true masterpiece. Its smoky, hearty, beefiness will keep you cozy during the chilly months of winter hibernation, while its crisp-clean-spicy finish will keep you refreshed on the sunniest of days in August. Smoke some fat, drink some whiskey, and impress your friends!

And believe us—your friends *will* be impressed (and probably drunk). Here are the recipes you'll need to make this cocktail, starting with the Sweet Dill Pickled Cipollini Onions for the garnish, the Smoked Suet Washed Booker's Bourbon, and the perfect combination of all these bold and beefy flavors to create the cocktail itself.

1 Sweet Dill Pickled Cipollini Onion

2 ounces Smoked Suet Washed Booker's Bourbon

¾ ounce Cynar

2 dashes Brooklyn Hemispherical Sriracha bitters

1. Chill your favorite coupe or martini glass.

2. Skewer a pickled onion with a frilled toothpick and set aside.

3. Fill a pint glass with ice and add all wet ingredients.

4. Stir with bar spoon. Freidus says you're stirring to "chill, waterize, and integrate the ingredients," all of which should be done to your own desired taste.

5. Strain into a chilled glass, either on the rocks or straight up (your choice). Garnish with the Sweet Dill Pickled Cipollini Onion.

STRAWBERRY SRIRACHA PUSH POPS

YIELD: 6 pops   START TO FINISH: 4 hours   ACTIVE TIME: 5 minutes

What's more fun than push pops? Order the push pop molds online (or grab some at a kitchen supply store) and whip these out of the freezer at your next backyard barbecue. They're inexpensive and infinitely reusable (until you inevitably lose one of the little pieces).

This type of eggless ice cream is known as "Philadelphia Style." It's fast and easy to prepare, and because there are no yolks involved, the sweet and rich flavors of the heavy cream really take the spotlight. Try this classic spin on a strawberry shake, but don't stop there. Use this recipe as a guide and create an endless amount of push pop flavors.

1 cup whole milk

¾ cup fresh strawberries, green stems removed

½ cup granulated sugar

1 tablespoon Red Rooster (page 148 or sriracha)

2 cups heavy cream

SPECIAL EQUIPMENT:

Ice cream maker

Push pop molds

1 Combine all ingredients except heavy cream in a blender and purée until evenly incorporated. Pour into a bowl, add heavy cream, and whisk together.

2 Spin mixture in an ice cream maker until it reaches a thick, soft serve-like consistency, about 15 minutes.

3 Quickly spoon into push pop containers, slap on the lid, and freeze for at least 4 hours before eating.

STORAGE NOTES: *Pops will keep in the freezer for up to two weeks.*

"MEZCAL MULE" COMPRESSED WATERMELON

Adapted from a cocktail by Jim Meehan of New York's PDT

YIELD: 1 boozed-up watermelon   START TO FINISH: 3¼ hours   ACTIVE TIME: 15 minutes

Imagine you're at an unassuming hot dog joint (Crif Dogs) in the East Village. Now imagine walking through a phone booth located inside said hot dog joint and entering one of NYC's most esteemed and "well-hidden" cocktail lounges. You've just entered PDT, an acronym for "Please Don't Tell" (oops, sorry), and it's one of the coolest places we've ever been.

What the hell does any of this have to do with boozy watermelon? Well, we adapted the concept for this recipe from a cocktail by Jim Meehan of PDT, who is responsible for one of the highest regarded bar programs in America. Meehan's Mezcal Mule has been deemed one of the best cocktails in Manhattan. Hopefully, this recipe will be what finally convinces you to buy that bottle of good mezcal you've always wanted to add to your liquor cabinet.

8 cups seedless watermelon
   (1 small watermelon), cut into
   1-inch cubes

6 ounces mezcal

1 ounce fresh ginger, peeled
   and thinly sliced

6 tablespoons freshly squeezed
   lime juice (about 3 limes)

Zest of 1 lime

3 ounces agave nectar

SPECIAL EQUIPMENT:

Vacuum food sealer

1 Evenly distribute all ingredients into 2 8-inch by 12-inch vacuum seal bags, and seal using a vacuum food sealer.

2 Refrigerate for at least 3 hours before serving up in a bowl or cups.

STORAGE NOTES: *Watermelon will keep in the refrigerator for up to three days.*

OLD FASHIONED SARSAPARILLA

YIELD: Approximately 2 liters   START TO FINISH: 3 hours   ACTIVE TIME: 15 minutes

When we set out to make this sarsaparilla, our good friend and bartender Daren Swisher recommended we use a 60/40 Demerara-to-granulated sugar ratio, and we fucking loved it.

This particular recipe uses a method of making simple syrup known as cold processing, which just means that heat is not applied to your sugar crystals as you transform them from a solid to a liquid. Cold processing puts the sugar molecules through a far gentler physical change than boiling does, preserving more of their caramel-like richness. The end result is a luscious, palate-coating creaminess that will give your soda some old fashioned warmth.

½ cup sassafras root

1 vanilla bean, split down the middle

16 green cardamom pods, gently crushed until open

2 cinnamon sticks

14 cloves

6 star anise pods

½ teaspoon kosher salt

4 cups water

1¾ cups Demerara sugar

1 cup granulated sugar

SPECIAL EQUIPMENT:

ISI Soda Siphon

Soda chargers, as needed

1 Bring all ingredients except sugar to a gentle simmer. Place lid on pot and simmer for 5 minutes, stirring occasionally.

2 Keep lid on pot, turn off heat, and steep for 1 hour.

3 Drain through fine mesh sieve. Cool liquid in refrigerator for at least 1 hour.

4 Add both sugars to infusion and stir with a spoon for 1 minute. Place mixture in blender and mix for 15 seconds.

5 Refrigerate until fully chilled before use.

6 Mix equal parts water with syrup, pour into your soda siphon, and carbonate with two charges. For best results, refrigerate overnight. (Devon Espinosa, Los Angeles cocktail guru, recommends overnight chilling to create the crisp, clean bubbliness that all great sodas embody.)

7 Siphon into chilled glass while soda is cold. No need for ice. Don't be scared of the frothy head. You want that.

STORAGE NOTES: *Syrup will keep in the refrigerator for up to ten days*

ACKNOWLEDGEMENTS

To the team at Union Park Press, who made all of this possible, understood our vision, and let us think we were getting away with more than we actually were. If it weren't for Deepa Chungi, Caitlin Cullerot, Shelby Larsson, Holly Gordon, and Nicole Vecchiotti, this cookbook would not be what it is. We are eternally grateful for all of your paper cuts, late nights, and greasy chins.

To all of our families and friends, who helped us more than they will ever know throughout the process, and the recipe testers for keeping us in line: Hope and Mark Chudy for letting us take over their house with props, burger propaganda, and general debauchery for the better part of a year; our beloved wives Astrid Bengtson and Katie Chudy; Samuel "Pops" Monsour Sr.; David and Nancy Barszcz; Sara, Chris, Emily, Erik, Kate, Beth and Matt; Janis and John a.k.a "Bubbles" and "Big Daddy;" Brian, Kathryn and Nora; Dylan and Keri Wise; Mark O'Leary; Patrick Maguire; Gary Goldblatt; Reuben Varzea; Peter Eco; Adrienne Chamberlain; Philip Preston, Jason Sayers and all the fine folks at PolyScience; Sana Goldberg and all the fine folks at Jacobsen Salt Co.; Jesse Black and the whole ThermoWorks team; Sandor Katz, for all amazing knowledge he's spread about fermentation (and for being an approachable guru!); Miroslaw "Mac" Stanuszek and the whole crew at The Sausage Maker; Inge and the whole team at Bradley Smoker; Brad and the entire family at Wasik's Cheese Shop in Wellesley, MA for all of the amazing cheese and generosity; Chris Coombs and The Boston Chops crew; Louis and Michael DiBiccari and everyone at Tavern Road; Steve "Nookie" Postal and the team at Commonwealth; Sammy Jackson and the KO Pies crew; Seth Freidus, Jen Fields, Michael Scelfo, Becca Arnold, David Tollerud and the Alden and Harlow crew; Joshua Smith and the Moody's Delicatessen and Provisions crew; Cabot Cheese; Bonnieview Farm; Plymouth Cheese; Grafton Village Cheese; King Arthur Flour; Daren Swisher; Dan Crothers; Kevin Clougher; Tony Susi; Blayne Daley; Tara Morris; Kari and Troy Schuler; Kerri Allard; Vanessa Yip; Jennifer Yukimura; Gabe Bellegard Bastos; MC Slim JB; Kyle Meekins; James DiSabatino; Rachel Leah Blumenthal; Amy McConnell; Jeff Gabel; Michael and Rebecca Robertson; Chris Tam; Daren Palacios; JB Morris; Kate Holowchik; Mark Lutz; Steven "Sexy Steve" Hacker; Kari and Michael Cooney. Matty "The Dude" Diekmann; Kristin and Jonathan Kay; Kelly Snogles; John Ross; Rachel and Drew Starr; and Joseph "Handsome Joe" Pritzky. Bill Leahy; Robyn Luongo and Mike Smith; Theresa "Tree" Yannetty; Tori and Mando; Leah Klein ; Darlene Coulombe; Aaron Gong ; Jen Jordan; Meghan Colloton; Mike and Emily Isman; Siphana Chau; Mike Dulock; Pamela Novinsky; Katie Quinn; Daniele Mathras and Bradley Fay; Dave Small; Tamara Tenenbaum; Joe Gatto; Paul Axel; Augustus Eustis; Brian Del Vecchio; Meghan Hargraves; Kay Benaroch; Sarah Keeping; Jim and Kiki Gross; Joan Cook; Jitti Chaithiraphant; and Cuzzy "Free" Laboda. Sara, Anil, Maya, Noah, and Jaime "Keystone" Ostrander.

COPYRIGHT TERMS

INDEX

Entries in bold are our featured burgers.